THE WORLD'S MAJOR
MILITARY JETS

Doug Richardson

MALLARD PRESS

A SALAMANDER BOOK

Mallard Press and its accompanying design and logo are
trademarks of BDD Promotional Book Company, Inc.

Mallard Press books are published in Australia by
Transworld Publishers (Aust) Pty Limited,
15-25 Helles Ave, Moorebank NSW 2170,
and in New Zealand by
Transworld Publishers (NZ) Limited,
Corner Moselle and Waipareira Avenues,
Henderson, Auckland.

© Salamander Books Ltd., 1991
129-137 York Way,
London N7 9LG,
England

ISBN 0-86325-100-6

CREDITS

Managing editor: Jilly Glassborow
Editor: Lindsay Peacock
Designer: Rachael Stone
Colour artwork: © Salamander Books
and © Pilot Press
Typeset by: SX Composing Ltd., England
Colour separation by: Scantrans Pte Ltd., Singapore
Printed by: Proost International Book Production,
Turnhout, Belgium

CONTENTS

INTRODUCTION

Air power is central to any military plan. Without friendly aircraft able to control the skies above an army or navy, the latter will be near-impotent. In 1973, Egypt realised that its air force was not able to match that of the Israelis, so the Egyptian forces that stormed across the Suez Canal in the opening stages of the Yom Kippur War relied on surface-to-air missiles to protect them from counter-attacks by the Israeli Air Force. The canal was successfully crossed but, without adequate air support, attempts to push forward and capture the strategic Gidi and Mitla passes failed.

Without the support of fighters able to deal with enemy aircraft, and attack aircraft able to strike powerful blows on enemy units in the front line of

Below: The futuristic shape of the YF-23 is a harbinger of things to come.

battle, modern ground and sea forces will have a hard time even to survive. With just two light aircraft carriers, the UK was only able to recapture the Falkland Islands in 1982 due to the fact that Argentinian fighters flying from their mainland bases were near the limits of their range. Like the Luftwaffe Bf109 fighters that escorted Heinkel and Dornier bombers in English skies during the Battle of Britain in 1940, the Mirages, Daggers and Skyhawks could spend only a short time in the combat zone before going home.

The aircraft in this book are the main combat types of the 1990s. Although air forces also have more specialised aircraft able to handle the maritime patrol, reconnaissance and bombing roles, no nation which faces a significant military threat can afford to be without one or more of the types that are described here.

Selecting the aircraft to be featured in a book such as this is bound to involve compromise. The goal here has been to show the fighters and attack aircraft which will be most important in the 1990s. As a result, some older fighters in service around the world have had to be omitted.

In the case of aircraft such as the Hunter, MiG-17, MiG-19 and F-104, this is because they are obsolete, in most cases serving in slowly decreasing numbers. Some Soviet types such as the Su-9/11, Su-15, Tu-128 and Yak-28 were omitted because they serve only with Soviet Air Force units tasked with home defence. In a world of diminishing tension between East and West, they are unlikely to ever see combat before they are scrapped.

Rather than feature such older aircraft, this book allocates space in its pages to the next generation of war-

planes – exotic machines such as the European Fighter Aircraft (EFA), Rafale D and JAS39 Gripen. India's Light Combat Aircraft (LCA) is in the same weight and performance class, but was excluded since details are sketchy and it is unlikely to fly until the late 1990s. In its place, India could deploy a new MiG fighter. Reported to be designated MiG-35, this combines an airframe derived from the MiG-21bis "Fishbed" with the engine used in the MiG-29 "Fulcrum".

Details of the USAF's new Advanced Tactical Fighters and the US Navy's planned A-12 Advanced Tactical Aircraft were not available when the book was written, but a photograph opposite shows one of the ATF designs – the Northrop/McDonnell Douglas YF-23. Like the rival Lockheed/ General Dynamics YF-22, this is a large and heavy aircraft incorporating stealth technology and powered by two advanced turbofan engines, each of which can deliver more than 30,000lb (13,600kg) of thrust. The General Dynamics/McDonnell Douglas A-12 will be a stealthy subsonic attack aircraft powered by the General Electric F404 turbofan.

Entering service in the late 1990s, these aircraft will serve well into the next century, as will many of the types discussed in this book, for despite improved East/West relations, all nations must maintain forces for defence. In view of that, combat jets will be with us for decades to come.

Above: For many nations, the combat-proven AIM-9 Sidewinder heat-seeking missile is the main air combat weapon.

Below: In-flight refuelling is vital for extending combat endurance or deployment to distant countries. Here, a Spanish Harrier II takes fuel during its delivery flight.

AERITALIA/AERMACCHI/EMBRAER AMX

Most nations are content to leave the ground-attack mission to obsolete fighters, but Italy and Brazil have developed this competent little strike aircraft as a custom-built solution. Powered by a single unreheated Spey turbofan, AMX can operate from short airstrips, takeoff and landing runs being around 1,650ft (500m) thanks to the high lift created by its double-slotted wing flaps.

Combat survivability is important in an aircraft which will attract ground fire, so AMX has two independent hydraulic systems, plus a "get you home" manual reversion mode.

Seven prototypes were built – three by Aeritalia, two by Aermacchi, and two by Embraer. The maiden flight was made in May 1984.

Each nation has devised its own avionics suite. On Italian aircraft, this is based on a Litton Italia INS, an Aeritalia computer-based weapon aiming system incorporating an Elta/FIAR Pointer ranging radar, and Elettronica active and passive EW systems. Brazilian aircraft have a simpler avionics suite based on the Technasa/SMA SCP-01 radar.

Italian aircraft carry an M61A1 20mm cannon on the port lower fuselage, while Brazil has installed two 30mm DEFA 554 cannon. Italian aircraft will rely on the AIM-9 Sidewinder for self-defence, while Brazilian aircraft will have that nation's MAA-1 Piranha missile. AMX can carry up to 8,377lb (3,800kg) of ordnance, much more than the older aircraft such as the G91.

Production started in 1986 and is slated to run until 1994. Under present plans 201 single-seaters and 51 two-seaters will be built for Italy, plus 69 single-seaters and 14 two-seaters for Brazil. Each part is made by only one company but both nations have their own assembly line.

SPECIFICATION: AMX
Role: Close-support/attack aircraft.
Length: 44ft 6.5in (13.57m).
Height: 15ft 0.25in (4.57m).
Wingspan: 29ft 1.5in (8.87m).
Weights: Empty, 14,770lb (6,700kg); loaded, 23,700lb (10,750kg); max. takeoff, 26,895lb (12,200kg).
Powerplant(s): One Rolls-Royce Spey Mk.807 turbofan.
Rating: 11,030lb (5,003kg).
Tactical radius: 280nm (370km) hi-lo-hi with 6,000lb (2,720kg) of ordnance.
Max. range: 1,600nm (2,965km).
Max. speed: Mach 0.86.
Ceiling: Not known.
Armament: One 20mm or two 30mm cannon plus 8,377lb (3,800kg) of ordnance.

Work on the AMX-T two-seater started in 1986, and the first example took to the sky for its maiden flight in 1990. The second cockpit is in the location used by the forward fuel tank of the basic aircraft. AMX-T is primarily intended to be employed as an operational trainer, but possible EW and maritime versions are envisaged. A single-seater fitted with a FIAR Grifo radar was used to test the feasibility of arming the latter variant with the Exocet anti-ship missile.

Above: The internationally-developed AMX strike fighter is currently flying in the markings of Brazil (front) and Italy (rear).

Below: Subsonic and relatively simple, the Spey-powered AMX was designed from the outset with combat survivability in mind.

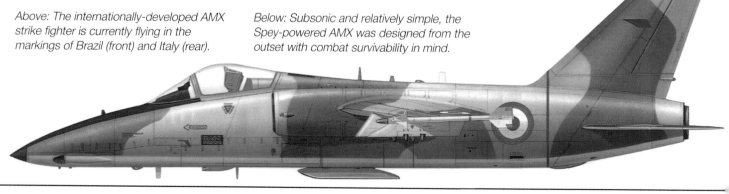

BRITISH AEROSPACE HARRIER & SEA HARRIER

SPECIFICATION: Sea Harrier FRS.2
Role: V/STOL naval fighter.
Length: 47ft 7in (14.50m).
Height: 12ft 2in (3.71m).
Wingspan: 25ft 3in (7.70m).
Weights: Empty, 14,052lb (6,374kg); loaded, c.19,000lb (8,600kg); max. takeoff, 26,200lb (11,880kg).
Powerplant(s): One Rolls-Royce Pegasus Mk.104 vectored-thrust turbofan.
Rating: 21,500lb (9,750kg).
Tactical radius: 400nm (750km) high-altitude interception sortie.
Max. range: 1,850nm (3,425km).
Max. speed: More than 640kts (1,185km/hr) at sea level; Mach 1.25 at altitude.
Ceiling: 51,200ft (15,600m).
Armament: 5,000lb (2,270kg) of ordnance, plus two 30mm Aden cannon.

For two decades from the late 1960s, the V/STOL Harriers of the Royal Air Force provided NATO with the only front-line fighter force not dependent on fixed runways. These long-serving aircraft are now at last giving way to the Harrier GR.5 which is basically an AV-8B Harrier II optimised for service with the RAF and which is examined on page 27.

As a result, few first generation Harrier GR.3s still serve with the RAF and most of those that do remain should be retired from front-line service within the next year or so.

In 1975 BAe was ordered to develop the Sea Harrier FRS.1 for service aboard the Royal Navy's Invincible-class light carriers. Intended to deal with long-range subsonic maritime patrol aircraft, it had a fighter-style canopy and Ferranti Blue Fox radar.

In 1982, every available Sea Harrier went to the South Atlantic for the war over the Falklands, where it accounted for 22 Argentinian aircraft. The Sea Harriers were augmented by a smaller number of RAF GR.3s. Although not designed for shipboard use, and flown by pilots with little experience of maritime operations, the GR.3s performed ground attack with conventional and laser-guided "smart" bombs.

BAe is now converting the Sea Harrier to FRS.2 standard, adding Blue Vixen pulse-Doppler multi-mode radar, an improved radar-warning receiver, a digital databus and HOTAS (hands-on-throttle-and-stick) controls. The rebuild adds a larger nose radome to house the bigger radar, extends the wingtips and stretches the rear fuselage while modified aircraft will also carry new missiles including the AIM-120A AMRAAM and British Aerospace's Sea Eagle and Alarm.

The sole export customer for the Sea Harrier was India, which operates a small force of Mk.51s (based on the FRS.1) from the aircraft carriers INS *Vikrant* and INS *Viraat* and a few T.60 two-seaters for training.

Below: Optimised for air defence, Royal Navy Sea Harrier FRS.1s are equipped with a nose-mounted Blue Fox multi-mode radar.

Above: An updated version of the original Harrier, the GR.3 is now being retired from the front-line by the RAF.

DASSAULT-BREGUET SUPER ETENDARD

SPECIFICATION: Super Etendard
Role: Shipboard strike fighter.
Length: 46ft 11.5in (14.31m).
Height: 12ft 8in (3.86m).
Wingspan: 31ft 6in (9.60m).
Weights: empty, 14,220lb (6,450kg); loaded, 20,280lb (9,200kg); max. takeoff, 25,350lb (11,500kg).
Powerplant(s): One Snecma Atar 8K-50 turbojet.
Rating: 11,025lb (5,000kg).
Tactical radius: 350nm (650km).
Max. range: More than 1,080nm (2,000km) with external fuel.
Max. speed: c. Mach 1 at altitude.
Ceiling: 45,000ft (13,700m).
Armament: up to 4,630lb (2,100kg) of ordnance, plus two 30mm DEFA cannon.

Above: Argentinian Navy Super Etendards took a heavy toll of British shipping in the 1982 war over the Falkland Islands.

By the late 1960s, the Dassault Etendard IVM fighter-bombers aboard the French Navy carriers *Foch* and *Clemenceau* were in need of replacement. In 1970, the Navy rejected the SEPECAT Jaguar M, but plans to acquire either the Vought A-7 or McDonnell Douglas A-4 were rejected in favour of a developed Etendard.

The structure of the aircraft was redesigned, a more powerful Atar 8K-50 replaced the older Atar 8, and the original austere avionics suite gave way to a new system based on a Thomson-CSF Agave multi-mode radar and a SAGEM-Kearfott inertial navigation and attack system. The end result was an all-new warplane which owed little to the original Etendard other than in general appearance.

First flight was in November 1977, and production deliveries were under way by the summer of 1978. In French service the aircraft can carry the AN52 nuclear bomb, and is now being modified to accept the ASMP supersonic cruise missile.

The 71 aircraft built for the French Navy were followed by a batch of 14 for the Argentinian Navy.

During the 1982 Falklands War, the Super Etendards could not be deployed aboard the Argentinian carrier *25 de Mayo*, since this had yet to be modernised. Equipped with newly-delivered Exocet anti-ship missiles, the aircraft operated from land bases, attacking and sinking the British guided-missile destroyer *Sheffield*, and the heavily laden container ship *Atlantic Conveyor*.

The production line closed on completion of the Argentinian order and attempts in the late 1980s to re-open it failed to attract further orders. In 1983, five French Navy Super Etendards were leased to Iraq pending delivery of that nation's Mirage F1 fighters. Armed with Exocet, these saw action over the Gulf starting in 1984, but were later returned to France.

Below: France's Aeronavale is the principle operator of the potent Super Etendard strike fighter. Armament can include Exocet as shown here or the ASMP nuclear missile.

DASSAULT-BREGUET MIRAGE III, 5 & 50/IAI KFIR

SPECIFICATION: Mirage IIIE
Role: Multi-role fighter.
Length: 49ft 3.5in (15.03m).
Height: 14ft 9in (4.50m).
Wingspan: 26ft 11.5in (8.22m).
Weights: Empty, 15,540lb (7,050kg); loaded, 21,165lb (9,600kg); max. takeoff, 30,200lb (13,700kg).
Powerplant(s): One Snecma Atar 9C, plus SEPR 844 rocket.
Rating: 13,227lb (6,000kg) with afterburning, plus 3,300lb (1,500kg) from rocket.
Tactical radius: 647nm (1,200km).
Max. range: 2,160nm (4,000km) with external fuel.
Max. speed: Mach 2.2.
Ceiling: 55,800ft (17,000m).
Armament: 8,810lb (4,000kg) of ordnance plus two 30mm DEFA cannon.

Above: Denied Mirage 5s by France, Israel reverse-engineered the aircraft to create the Kfir (Lion Cub). This US Marine Corps example was used for air combat training.

In 1961, the French Air Force took delivery of the first production examples of its first Mach 2 fighter – Dassault's delta-winged Mirage IIIC. It was to be the start of a long production run which was destined to stretch into the 1990s.

For many air arms around the world, this cost-effective multi-role fighter proved ideal. The improved Mirage IIIE was optimised for the strike role, but for air forces prepared to sacrifice avionics for fuel and lower cost, Dassault created the needle-nosed Mirage 5. This sold even better than the III, but the Mirage 50 (an aircraft fitted with the more powerful engine used in the Mirage F1) was far less successful.

More than half the air forces that use the Mirage III, 5 and 50 have embarked on schemes to update the aircraft. Most involve new avionics, but the schemes adopted by Brazil, Chile, South Africa, Spain and Switzerland involve the addition of foreplanes that are intended to bestow enhanced manoeuvrability qualities.

Dassault had experimented with foreplanes in the late 1960s, but the concept was popularised in the late 1970s by Israel's Kfir C2, an unlicensed Mirage copy powered by the General Electric J79 engine. Many of the 185 built were converted to the C7 standard. Introduced in 1983, this has an uprated engine, a HOTAS (hands-on-throttle-and-stick) cockpit and two extra stores stations. Production of the Kfir has ended, but tooling is intact. Some have been exported and Israel is now planning to re-engine others with the Atar in order to overcome US export restrictions.

In December 1982, Dassault flew the canard-equipped Mirage 3NG. This had a new fly-by-wire (FBW) control system, and Mirage 2000-style relaxed stability, but no customers emerged. The company now offers the canard-equipped but non-FBW Mirage 50M.

Below: The French Air Force is rapidly phasing out its Mirage IIIE fleet, but export models of the delta-winged fighter will serve around the world until the late 1990s.

DASSAULT-BREGUET MIRAGE F1

SPECIFICATION: Mirage F1C
Role: Interceptor.
Length: 50ft 2.5in (15.3m).
Height: 14ft 9in (4.5m).
Wingspan: 27ft 6.75in (8.40m).
Weights: empty, 16,310lb (7,400kg); loaded, 24,030lb (10,900kg); max. takeoff, 35,715lb (16,200kg).
Powerplant(s): One Snecma Atar 9K-50.
Rating: 15,873lb (7,200kg) with afterburning.
Tactical radius: 230 – 750nm (420 – 1,390km) hi-lo-hi.
Max. range: 1,782nm (3,300km) with external fuel.
Max. speed: Mach 2.2.
Ceiling: 65,600ft (20,000m).
Armament: 13,900lb (6,300kg) of ordnance plus two 30mm DEFA cannon.

The delta wing is easy to manufacture, but is not the ideal wing for a fighter. Drag is high when manoeuvring, while the high nose-up angle needed to maintain lift at low speeds higher than those of a swept-wing aircraft make the takeoff and landing runs uncomfortably long.

By the early 1960s, Dassault engineers had devised economical methods of building a swept wing, using this first for the heavy two-seat

Below: By adding a flight-refuelling probe to some Mirage F1s, the French Air Force came up with a fighter that can undertake long-range overseas deployments.

Mirage F2 fighter, then for a lighter single-seat design able to replace the Mirage III. The French Air Force abandoned the F2, switching its order to the smaller and cheaper aircraft, which entered service in quantity during 1973.

Compared with the delta-winged Mirages, it could pull about 1g more when manoeuvring, carried 40 per cent more fuel, had lower takeoff and landing speeds and used shorter airstrips. Add to these improvements a multi-mode Cyrano IV or IVM radar, Matra R.550 "dogfight" missiles, good handling qualities and a reputation which it shared with the deltas of being a "pilot's aircraft" and it's not hard to see why the type was a great export success. Like the Mirage III, 5 and 50, it was to remain in quantity production into the 1990s.

Final version for the French Air Force was the F1CR-200 reconnaissance aircraft, which had a flight refuelling probe, but 55 F1Cs are being

updated to F1CT standard, receiving better air-to-ground capability. Addition of a refuelling probe converts a French Air Force F1C into an F1C-200 and refuelling probes have also been adopted by Iraq, Libya, Morocco, South Africa and Spain.

Other models are the F1A ground-attack aircraft, F1B and F1D two-seat trainers and the F1E multi-role version. Export versions of the F1C have a radar based on the Cyrano IV or IVM while the F1E has the Cyrano IVMR.

The F1 has seen combat with the Iraqi and South African air forces, but few details are available. Iraqi F1s fired more than 100 Exocet missiles during the Iran/Iraq war, one of which hit the US frigate *Stark*.

Below: In addition to pure fighter versions, the French Air Force operates a sizeable force of reconnaissance-dedicated F1CR-200s. The examples below wear desert camouflage colours for operations over North-West Africa.

DASSAULT-BREGUET MIRAGE 2000

Originally studied as a private venture in the mid-1970s, this agile fighter combines the proven delta concept with relaxed stability, a fly-by-wire (FBW) control system, the M53 engine originally developed for the proposed Mach 2.7 Super Mirage and France's first airborne pulse-Doppler radar system.

First flight of a Mirage 2000 was on 10 March 1978, but development then proved more difficult than had been anticipated. Not until 1984 was the first squadron officially formed and even it had to make up its initial strength with aircraft borrowed from trials units. As export customers emerged, aircraft under construction were diverted from the French Air Force to the export market, slowing French deployment.

Basic model is the 2000C interceptor. The 2000B is a two-seat trainer while the 2000R is for reconnaissance. Problems with the Thomson-CSF RDI radar planned for use on French Air Force Mirage 2000Cs forced installation of the lower-grade RDM export radar on initial service aircraft, while the full-specification engine did not enter service in French 2000Cs until 1987, with export users and the 2000N fleet having priority.

The 2000N is a two-seat nuclear strike aircraft fitted with an ESD Antilope V radar for terrain following, Thomson-CSF colour CRT, plus two SAGEM inertial platforms, and equipped with the ASMP supersonic cruise missile. Currently cleared for automatic terrain-following flight at 300ft (90m), it will eventually operate at lower altitudes. A total of 75 is planned, plus 105 2000D – a similar aircraft that cannot carry ASMP but can carry conventional weapons.

Below: The latest member of the Mirage family is proving equally versatile and has spawned the nuclear-capable 2000N model able to carry the ASMP cruise missile.

SPECIFICATION: Mirage 2000C
Role: Air-superiority fighter.
Length: 47ft 1.25in (14.36m).
Height: 17ft 0.75in (5.20m).
Wingspan: 29ft 11.5in (9.13m).
Weights: Empty, 16,534lb (7,500kg); loaded, 23,940lb (10,860kg); max. takeoff, 37,480lb (17,000kg).
Powerplant(s): One Snecma M53-P2 turbofan.
Rating: 14,462lb (6,560kg) dry thrust, 21,385lb (9,700kg) with afterburning.
Tactical radius: Over 400nm (740km).
Max. range: 1,800nm (3,335km) with external fuel.
Max. speed: Mach 2.2.
Ceiling: 59,000ft (18,000m).
Armament: 13,890lb (6,300kg) of ordnance, plus two 30mm DEFA cannon.

Newer versions under development for the 1990s include the 2000-3 with advanced cockpit displays, the 2000-5 with the Thomson-CSF RDY radar, a holographic HUD and able to carry MICA missiles, plus the 2000S export version of the 2000D.

Below: Air-to-air missiles extend the reach of the agile Mirage 2000C interceptor. This French Air Force example carries Magic 2 dogfight missiles on the outboard pylons as well as the heavier radar-guided Super 530.

13

DASSAULT-BREGUET RAFALE D & M

> **SPECIFICATION: Rafale D**
> **Role:** Multi-role fighter.
> **Length:** 49ft 2in (14.98m).
> **Height:** 16ft 9in (5.1m).
> **Wingspan:** 35ft 2in (10.72m).
> **Weights:** Empty, 18,960lb (8,600kg); loaded, 28,200lb (12,800kg); max. takeoff, 40,100lb (18,200kg).
> **Powerplant(s):** Two Snecma M88-15 turbofans.
> **Rating:** 16,530 lb (7,500kg) with afterburning.
> **Tactical radius:** 300-500nm (556-926km).
> **Max. range:** Not known.
> **Max. speed:** Mach 2.
> **Ceiling:** Not known.
> **Armament:** Up to 14,300lb (6,500kg) of ordnance, plus internal cannon.

To its supporters, Rafale is a potential world-beater which will match the export success of the Mirage III, 5 and F1. Others see it as an over-expensive luxury – an "abyss for billions" which France cannot afford. One thing is certain, if committed to production, Rafale will be the "hottest" Western fighter other than the USAF's planned YF-22 or YF-23.

Below: Though outwardly similar to the first prototype, the definitive production Rafale D will be a refined design, taking advantage of some aspects of stealth technology.

To prove the basic design, Dassault-Breguet flew the F404-powered Rafale A technology demonstrator in 1986. Two production versions are planned – Rafale D for the French Air Force and Rafale M for service on French carriers. Both will be smaller and lighter than the Rafale A while SNECMA's new 16,860lb (7,648kg) M88-2 turbofan will provide greater installed thrust.

Wingspan will be 34ft 9.25in (10.6m) and length 50ft 10.25in (15.5m). Empty weight of the D version is expected to be 18,960lb (8,600kg), while the M should be 20,280lb (9,199kg).

The greater weight of the M is due to features needed to make the aircraft suitable for carrier operations – a more rugged undercarriage with a twin-wheel nosegear and the ability to cope with a 21ft/sec (6.5m/sec) descent rate on landing. Carbonfibre technology rules out folding wings.

Five prototypes will be built – a two-seat D, single-seat M, a single-seat D, another single-seat M and a final two-seater. The first is due to fly during early 1991. Production should begin in 1994, allowing the aircraft to enter operational service with the French Air Force in the course of 1996.

Maximum warload will be more than 7,700lb (3,493kg). Maximum takeoff weight on an air-defence mission should be 30,865lb (14,000kg), rising to 44,092lb (20,000kg) on strike missions. Combat radius on strike missions will be in the region of 300-350nm (556-648 km).

Below: To prove the technology needed for the eventual production aircraft, Dassault flew the prototype Rafale with a pair of General Electric F404 turbofans. Later, this aircraft was used to test the SNECMA M88 engine.

EUROFIGHTER EFA

SPECIFICATION: EFA.
Role: Multi-role fighter.
Length: 44ft 10in (13.65m).
Height: Not known.
Wingspan: 34ft 5in (10.5m).
Weights: Empty, 21,500lb (9,750kg); loaded, not known; max. takeoff, 37,480lb (17,000kg).
Powerplant(s): Two Eurojet EJ200 turbofans.
Rating: 20,000lb (9,070kg) in afterburner.
Tactical radius: 250 – 300nm (460 – 550km).
Max. range: Not known.
Max. speed: Greater than Mach 1.8.
Ceiling: Not known.
Armament: Six air-to-air missiles plus an internal cannon.

Above: The technology demonstrator for the Eurofighter project was the British Aerospace EAP. This was fitted with Turbo-Union RB.199 engines but the production aircraft will have Eurojet EJ.200 turbofans.

In 1983 several West European air forces drew up an outline staff target for a next-generation fighter. By the mid-1990s, the end product could be squadrons of Eurofighters in service with the air forces of Germany, Italy, Spain and the UK.

France was to have been a partner in the programme, but pulled out in July 1985, a year after the start of feasibility studies, when it became obvious that the other partners were unwilling to accept the low target weight which France thought would lead to a good export aircraft.

Eurofighter Gmbh was formed in June 1986 to manage the programme. Development contracts for the aircraft and its 20,000lb (9,072kg) thrust Eurojet EJ200 engine were awarded in November 1989 and work has started on eight prototypes. The first two will be powered by the RB.199. Others will have the EJ200, the first to fly with this being a two-seater. Built by the UK, it should be airborne in 1992.

If full production of EFA goes ahead as planned, this will involve 250 for Germany, 165 for Italy, 100 for Spain and 250 for the UK. Included in this total would be around 100 two-seaters to meet training requirements.

The avionics suite will include a GEC Ferranti radar with a range of 50-80nm (92-148km) and the ability to track eight targets at once, a powerful Defensive Aids Sub-System (DASS) EW installation, a navigation system based on laser INS and a GPS satellite navigation receiver, plus an advanced HUD, three large multi-function colour displays and, probably, an advanced helmet sight.

A total of 15 hardpoints will be provided for ordnance like advanced guided missiles, while a single 27mm cannon will be carried internally.

Below: For Germany, Italy, Spain and the United Kingdom production of the Eurofighter will be a most expensive venture and may fall victim to cuts or cancellation as defence spending falls.

FAIRCHILD A-10 THUNDERBOLT II

SPECIFICATION: A-10A Thunderbolt II.
Role: Close support aircraft.
Length: 53ft 4in (16.26m).
Height: 14ft 8in (4.47m).
Wingspan: 57ft 6in (17.6m).
Weights: Empty, 21,541lb (9,771kg); loaded, 31,831lb (14,438kg); max. takeoff, 50,000lb (22,680kg).
Powerplant(s): Two General Electric TF34-GE-100 turbofans.
Rating: 9,065lb (4,111kg).
Tactical radius: 540nm (1,000km).
Max. range: 2,131nm (3,949km).
Max. speed: 450kts (834km/hr).
Ceiling: Not known.
Armament: One GAU-8/A 30mm cannon plus 14,340lb (6,500kg) of ordnance.

This strange-looking aircraft may be considered a legacy from the Vietnam War. Its relevance to the 1990s or even the 1980s is questionable and the USAF now seems to be determined to hustle it into retirement as soon as decently possible.

Development of an armoured attack aircraft was ordered in 1967. Following a long period of studies, rival Northrop YA-9 and Fairchild YA-10 prototypes were flight tested in 1972 and the latter design was selected for production in early 1973. Deliveries were too late for

Below: Although the A-10A can carry AGM-65D Maverick missiles, these are an expensive way of killing a tank. The 30mm Avenger cannon is more cost-effective.

the Vietnam War and this huge aircraft found itself being deployed to Western Europe as a specialised "tank-buster".

With widely-spaced engines, triplicated wing and tail spars, well-separated and protected fuel lines and control runs and a "bathtub" of armour around the cockpit, the A-10 is designed to cope with hits by shells of up to 23mm calibre.

It can carry AGM-65D Maverick infra-red homing missiles, but its main anti-tank weapon is the massive 30mm GAU-8/A cannon mounted within the fuselage. This seven-barrelled gun can spew out 70 rounds per second – subcalibre dart projectiles made from depleted uranium, able to punch a way through the side or top armour of main battle tanks. The 1,350-round magazine has enough capacity for ten two-second bursts of fire.

The wisdom of operating an aircraft the size of a World War 2 B-25 Mitchell medium bomber at low level over a SAM-infested battlefield seems questionable and all attempts to market the aircraft outside of the USA failed. In combat, this slow-moving machine would be vulnerable to attack by even an obsolete fighter such as the MiG-17 "Fresco".

In the late 1970s, Fairchild created a single private-venture prototype of a two-seat night/all-weather version. Equipped with WX-50 radar and AAR-42 forward-looking infra-red

Above: An A-10 formation starts its descent to the treetop heights which are its natural combat environment. At altitude, it would be vulnerable to aircraft or missile attack.

systems, it was able to operate in visibility of less than a mile (1.6km) and under cloud ceilings of down to 300ft (90m), but the USAF rejected it.

In the 1980s, the aircraft was earmarked to carry the LANTIRN day/night navigation and attack system, but this costly hardware will now only be installed on some F-16s and the two-seat F-15E. The USAF now wants to deploy a close-support version of the F-16 and NATO force reductions should see most front-line A-10s retired by 1993.

GENERAL DYNAMICS F-16 FIGHTING FALCON

SPECIFICATION: F-16C Fighting Falcon.
Role: Air combat fighter.
Length: 49ft 3in (15.01m).
Height: 16ft 8.5in (5.09m).
Wingspan: 31ft 0in (9.45m).
Weights: Empty, 18,238lb (8,273kg); loaded, 25,071lb (11,372kg); max. takeoff, 42,300lb (19,184kg).
Powerplant(s): One Pratt & Whitney F100-PW-220 turbofan.
Rating: 23,770lb (10,780kg) in afterburner.
Tactical radius: Over 500nm (925km).
Max. range: More than 2,100nm (3,890km) with external tanks.
Max. speed: Greater than Mach 2.
Ceiling: More than 50,000ft (15,240m).
Armament: AIM-7 and AIM-9 missiles, one 20mm cannon and 12,000lb (5,440kg) of ordnance.

When this small fighter was selected for USAF and NATO service in the mid-1970s, some observers (including the writer) feared that it would prove to be a 1980s equivalent to the F-104G, a high-performance aircraft which would prove tricky to fly and expensive to maintain. They were wrong. The F-16 has emerged as one of the classic warplanes of its generation and its avail-

Below: The markings on this heavily-laden F-16A are of the 388th Tactical Fighter Wing which introduced the type to service.

ability on the export market did much to spoil the sales record of its nearest Western rival – the Mirage 2000.

By accepting the cost of funding rival GD YF-16 and Northrop YF-17 demonstrators, the USAF gave the designers of both aircraft freedom to flight test new technology. The GD team decided to adopt relaxed stability, combining an inherently unstable airframe with a fly-by-wire control system that would be able to cope with the resulting flying characteristics.

The result is what aircraft designers nickname a "slippery ship" – an aircraft whose "tamed" instability results in superb manoeuvrability. In the 1980s and 1990s, this seems the logical way to design a fighter, but for the mid-1970s it was an act of technological daring, as was the use of a sidestick

controller and a reclining seat devised to increase the pilot's tolerance to the rigorous g forces of air combat.

The original F100-powered F-16A single-seater and F-16B two-seat production versions have since been followed by the F-16C and F-16D respectively, models which can use either the Pratt & Whitney F100 or the General Electric F110. In the mid-1980s, the latter engine offered more thrust so was often specified by export customers. GD has proposed various improved Agile Falcon versions, but the only firm "super F-16" project currently under way is Japan's canard-equipped Mitsubishi FS-X.

Below: The F-16's high performance and fairly reasonable price has won it many orders. This example is for Indonesia.

GENERAL DYNAMICS F-111

SPECIFICATION: F-111F
Role: Heavy strike fighter.
Length: 75ft 6.5in (23.03m).
Height: 17ft 0.5in (5.19m).
Wingspan: 31ft 11.5in (9.74m) swept; 63ft 0in (19.2m) unswept.
Weights: Empty, 47,481lb (21,537kg); max. takeoff, 100,000lb (45,369kg).
Powerplant(s): Two Pratt & Whitney TF30-P-100 turbofans.
Rating: 25,100lb (11,385kg) with afterburning.
Tactical radius: 1,500nm (2,780km) hi-lo-hi.
Max. range: More than 3,400nm (6,297km).
Max. speed: Mach 2.5 at altitude.
Ceiling: 45,000ft (13,700m).
Armament: Up to 28,000lb (12,799kg) of ordnance, plus one 20mm cannon.

Few combat aircraft programmes can have generated quite so much political controversy and media criticism as the F-111. The result of a 1961 decision by the US Defense Secretary to order the USAF and US Navy to develop a common fighter, the F-111 emerged as an effective low-level strike bomber – which is what the USAF actually wanted in the first place.

The USN experience was less happy. Unlike the USAF, it was looking for a fighter, but the short-lived

Below: European-based F-111Fs of the 48th TFW have the Pave Tack pod under the fuselage. This IR imager can designate targets for attack by laser-guided weapons.

F-111B interceptor was too heavy to meet the requirement. After only a handful of prototypes had been built, the F-111B was cancelled.

The USAF's F-111A was the first operational variable-geometry aircraft and the first equipped for automatic terrain-following flight. Although shorter in range than had been demanded by the specification and prone to engine problems, it was the best strike aircraft of its day, entering service in 1967.

No-one was prepared to stop the production line until the type's shortcomings could be sorted out, so the F-111A was followed by a series of gradually-improving versions – the F-111D, E, and F, then the FB-111A version for Strategic Air Command. Each had its own unique combination of avionics, engine and inlet systems. Australia took much-delayed delivery of 24 F-111Cs in the early 1970s, while the UK ordered 50 F-111Ks in 1965, only to cancel the deal three years later as a cost-saving measure.

Most of the F-111A fleet was rebuilt in the early 1980s by Grumman. Known as the EF-111A Raven, these now carry a complex suite of EW systems and are deployed as stand-off or escort jamming aircraft. Around 380 D, E and F models are being modified with updated avionics, including new terrain-following and attack radars, so maintenance should be simplified for the remainder of the aircraft's career.

Like the F-111C and the cancelled F-111K, SAC's FB-111A has the long-span wing originally developed for the F-111B fighter. Fielded as a partial replacement for the B-58 and early-model B-52s, these are no longer needed as strategic bombers and are to be modified to F-111G standard and re-assigned to Tactical Air Command for use in conventional and tactical nuclear strike roles.

Below: More than 20 years after entering USAF service, the F-111 is still a most effective warplane. These F-111Ds are from the 27th TFW at Cannon AFB, New Mexico.

GRUMMAN A-6 INTRUDER

In the mid-1950s, the US Marine Corps needed a new low-level bomber able to attack targets in all weather by day or night, but the subsonic attack bomber developed for this task was born several years too early for its own good. The electronics technology needed to handle the navigation and attack tasks was in its infancy, while many potentially useful advances in airframe and propulsion technology were not ready for incorporation into a service aircraft.

Instead of fuel-efficient turbofans, the A-6 Intruder (then known as the A2F Intruder) had to make do with J52 turbojets, while its wing had to be large enough to generate sufficient lift for carrier operations without the aid of flap blowing or other lift-enhancing aids. The aircraft's sophisticated DIANE (Digital Integrated Attack Navigation Equipment) avionics suite was designed when complexity was directly proportional to unreliability.

When the aircraft entered service in 1963, keeping its avionics operational proved difficult but the US Navy was equal to the task and the A-6 was committed to the Vietnam War, flying its

Below: TRAM gear gives the A-6E the ability to examine targets detected by radar and then "mark" them with laser energy.

first combat sorties in July 1965. By 1966, avionics designed for terrain-following flight at 300ft (90m) were coping with flight at 100ft (30m).

With effect from the mid-1970s, the early-model A-6A, B and C versions gradually gave way to the definitive A-6E. Solid-state electronics replaced earlier vacuum-tube systems, while the separate search and tracking radars were replaced by a single multi-mode set, making the aircraft easier to fly and simpler to maintain.

Many earlier aircraft have been rebuilt to the A-6E standard, while 1974 saw the appearance of the TRAM (Target Recognition and Attack Multisensor), contained in a turret fitted under the nose of the aircraft.

In 1987 Grumman flew the A-6F, a new version with unreheated F404 turbofan engines and a completely

Below: A strong structure and rugged J52 turbojet engines plus a modern nav/attack system make Intruder the world's most effective carrier-based bomber.

SPECIFICATION: A-6E Intruder
Role: Carrier-based attack bomber.
Length: 54ft 9in (16.69m).
Height: 16ft 2in (4.93m).
Wingspan: 53ft 0in (16.15m).
Weights: Empty, 26,746lb (12,132kg); max. takeoff, 58,600lb (26,580kg).
Powerplant(s): Two Pratt & Whitney J52-P-8B turbojets.
Rating: 9,300lb (4,218kg).
Tactical radius: 765nm (1,415km) hi-lo-hi.
Max. range: 2,818nm (5,222km) with max external fuel.
Max. speed: 560kts (1,037km/hr) at sea level.
Ceiling: 42,400ft (12,900m).
Armament: Up to 18,000lb (8,165kg) of ordnance.

new avionics suite, but Congress refused to pay for production aircraft. The A-6E will eventually be replaced by the new A-12 Advanced Tactical Aircraft when this becomes available in the late 1990s. In the meantime, some Intruders are to be retrofitted with a composite wing to eliminate fatigue problems.

GRUMMAN F-14 TOMCAT

Developed to replace the US Navy's F-4 Phantoms, Tomcat flew for the first time in December 1970. Development was swift by modern standards, since the TF30 turbofan engines, AWG-9 radar and long-range AIM-54 Phoenix missiles were already under development for the unsuccessful F-111B interceptor.

When the aircraft entered service in 1972, it carried the longest ranged fighter radar and air-to-air missiles in the world, a record which remains valid almost two decades later.

Sole export customer was Iran, which took delivery of 80. Following the Iranian revolution and the seizure of the US embassy and its diplomats, the supply of spares was cut off, but the Iranian aircraft did see some action during the Iraq/Iran war.

Above: Tomcat will probably be the last USN-developed fighter. Its replacement will be a navalised version of the USAF's ATF.

SPECIFICATION: F-14A Tomcat
Role: Carrier-based fighter.
Length: 62ft 8in (19.10m).
Height: 16ft 0in (4.88m).
Wingspan: 64ft 1.5in (19.54m) unswept; 38ft 2.5in (11.65m) swept.
Weights: Empty, 40,104lb (18,191kg); loaded, 58,715lb (26,632kg); max. takeoff, 74,349lb (33,724kg).
Powerplant(s): Two Pratt & Whitney TF30-PW-414 afterburning turbofans.
Rating: 20,900lb (9,480kg) in afterburner.
Tactical radius: Not known.
Max. range: c.1,735nm (3,220km).
Max. speed: Mach 1.2 at low level; Mach 2.34 at altitude.
Ceiling: Above 50,000ft (15,240m).
Armament: Sidewinder, Sparrow and Phoenix missiles, plus 20mm cannon.

Two improvements were devised in the early 1980s. One was a new suite of avionics, including an APG-71 radar, and Infra-Red Search and Tracking (IRST) chin sensor, the Advanced Self-Protection Jammer, the ALR-67 threat-warning system and a JTIDS datalink. The other was replacement of the TF30 engines with the higher-thrust General Electric F110.

Both changes were planned for the F-14D, but the new engine was ready ahead of the avionics. As a result, production was switched in 1987 to the re-engined F-14A Plus. Congress proved unwilling to fund large-scale production of the F-14D, forcing the USN to draw up a scheme to create this aircraft by rebuilding existing F-14As.

At present, the USN is due to deploy a navalised version of the USAF's Advanced Tactical Fighter (ATF) in the late 1990s. As an alternative, Grumman has proposed Tomcat 21, an aircraft with upgraded F-14D avionics, the 29,000lb (13,154kg) thrust F110 Improved Performance Engine, new glove sections containing an extra 2,500lb (1,134kg) of fuel and a modified high-lift flap system.

Below: As fighters go, Tomcat is big, but no other US or Soviet aircraft can match its powerful radar and long-range missiles.

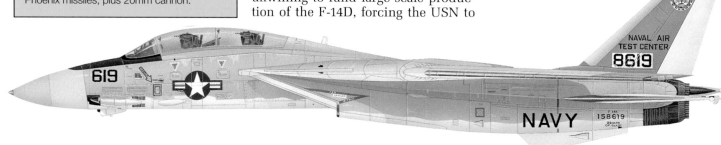

IAR-93/SOKO ORAO

Developed by the aircraft industries of Romania and Jugoslavia, this small strike fighter can be thought of as a low-tech mini-Jaguar. In fact, it's probably the sort of aircraft Jaguar might have been had France not agreed to collaborate with the UK in developing its fighter-bomber of the 1970s. This resemblance is more than skin deep. Not only does it look like Jaguar, but it also uses a modified version of the Jaguar undercarriage.

Prototypes of the single-seater flew in both countries within 20 minutes of each other on 31 October 1974. Two-seat prototypes followed in both countries in January 1977.

Below: Creation of the definitive version of the Orao was delayed by problems with the afterburning engines. This prototype was used to prove the new powerplant.

The original versions of the aircraft used locally-built licenced copies of the Rolls-Royce Viper turbojet, but in this form the aircraft was somewhat underpowered. The Romanian IAR-93A version entered production in 1979, making its first flight in 1981. Twenty were built, a mixture of single and two-seaters. The equivalent Jugoslavian model was the Orao 1, which appeared in 1980.

Once the locally-developed afterburning Viper was ready for use, Jugoslavia flew the Orao 2 single-seat strike aircraft in October 1983, then the Orao 2D two-seater trainer in July 1986. A total of 100 Orao 2s and 2Ds was ordered and all Orao 1 two-seaters have been rebuilt to 2D standard. Romania's IAR-93B made its first flight in 1985. Single and two-seat forms exist, 165 having been ordered.

> **SPECIFICATION:** IAR-93A.
> **Role:** Strike fighter.
> **Length:** 48ft 10.5in (14.90m).
> **Height:** 14ft 7.25in (4.45m).
> **Wingspan:** 31ft 6.75in (9.62m).
> **Weights:** Empty, 13,558lb (6,150kg); loaded, 19,458lb (8,826kg); max. takeoff, 22,765lb (10,326kg).
> **Powerplant(s):** Two licence-built Rolls-Royce Viper Mk632-41R turbojets.
> **Rating:** 4,000lb (1,814kg).
> **Tactical radius:** 194nm (360km) with maximum ordnance.
> **Max. range:** Not known.
> **Max. speed:** 577kts (1,070km/hr) at low level.
> **Ceiling:** 34,450ft (10,500m).
> **Armament:** 3,307lb (1,500kg) of ordnance plus two 23mm GSh-23L cannon.

Manufacturing work is split between the SOKO plant at Mostar, which makes the aft fuselage, wings and vertical fin, and CNIAR at Craiova in Romania, responsible for the forward and centre fuselage sections as well as the horizontal tail surfaces. Assembly of the aircraft is performed by factories in both countries.

Below: In its basic form with non-augmented engines, Orao proved satisfactory but underpowered. Efforts to export the type have failed to meet with any success.

LOCKHEED F-117A

SPECIFICATION: F-117A "Senior Trend".
Role: reconnaissance/strike fighter.
Length: 65ft 11in (20.09m).
Height: 12ft 5in (3.78m).
Wingspan: 43ft 4in (13.21m).
Weights: Empty, c.30,000lb (13,800kg); loaded, c.48,000lb (21,800kg); max. takeoff, 52,500lb (23,800kg).
Powerplant(s): Two non-afterburning General Electric F404-GE-F1D2 turbo fans.
Rating: 10,800-12,500lb (4,900-5,670kg).
Tactical radius: 800-1,200nm (1,500-2,200km).
Max. range: Not known.
Max. speed: High subsonic.
Ceiling: Not known.
Armament: c.4,000lb (1,800kg) of stores carried internally.

Development of the F-117A stealth fighter started in 1978, following flight trials with the smaller XST technology demonstration aircraft. First flight was in 1981 and deliveries to Tactical Air Command started in the following year, allowing the aircraft to become operational in 1983.

The aircraft is made from aluminium alloy, over which tiles of radar-absorbing material (RAM) are applied. The basic shape is made of flat surfaces, a technique known as faceting. This tend to reflect radar energy in narrow beams, scattering it in militarily-useless directions.

The fuselage sides are steeply sloped, while the sharply-swept wing and tail surfaces have prismatic aerofoils made up of flat surfaces. Control is by inboard and outboard elevons, plus an all-moving V tail.

Above: Lockheed's F-117A first flew in 1981 and entered service in 1983 but good quality photographs were not released until 1990.

Each inlet is divided into two sections, screened by a grille with individual mesh sections measuring around 1in by 0.6in (2.5cm by 1.5cm). This is designed to prevent radar energy from entering the inlet and being reflected from its interior and the front face of the engines.

Engine efflux is probably mixed with surplus air from the oversized inlets before being released from two 12ft (3.65m) wide slot outlets on the rear fuselage, forming flat "beaver-tail" plumes, which allows the gases to cool more rapidly than in a circular jet.

Two electro-optical systems are used for target detection and laser illumination. One is in a cavity just below the front panel of the canopy, the other in a similar cavity on the belly of the aircraft.

Details of the aircraft remained secret until 1988, a result of its operating only by night from Tonopah, Nevada. Several took part in the December 1989 US invasion of Panama. From early 1990 onwards, it was gradually declassified. A total of 59 was eventually built by Lockheed's celebrated "Skunk Works" before the last example was handed over to the 37th Tactical Fighter Wing at Tonopah in July 1990.

Below: Probably the ugliest aircraft in the book, the F-117A has an angular shape that is dictated by the rules of stealth technology.

McDONNELL DOUGLAS F-4 PHANTOM

SPECIFICATION: F-4E Phantom II.
Role: Multi-role fighter.
Length: 62ft 11in (19.17m).
Height: 16ft 3in (4.96m).
Wingspan: 38ft 5in (11.70m).
Weights: Empty, 29,535lb (13,397kg); max. takeoff, 61,795lb (28,030kg).
Powerplant(s): Two General Electric J79-GE-17 turbojets.
Rating: 11,870lb (5,384kg) dry thrust, 17,900lb (8,119kg) with afterburning.
Tactical radius: 700nm (1,295km) combat air patrol with external fuel.
Max. range: c.2,000nm (3,700km).
Max. speed: Mach 2.2.
Ceiling: 56,120ft (17,100m).
Armament: 16,000lb (7,250kg) of ordnance, plus one 20mm M61 cannon.

Above: A USAF F-4E releases a GBU-15 Modular Glide Bomb. An IR seeker will guide the weapon to impact.

In the three decades since the F-4 Phantom first entered service, the type has scored more than 280 combat "kills", including around 100 MiG-21s. The aircraft first flew in 1958 and deliveries started in 1961. Older models have mostly been retired. The most common types in service are the widely-exported F-4E (first version to carry an internal cannon), the F-4F used by Germany, Japan's F-4EJ, and Britain's Spey-engined F-4K and F-4M. Specialised models include the RF-4C and RF-4E for reconnaissance and the F-4G "Wild Weasel".

Below: Vietnam-style camouflage is worn by this US Air Force F-4E but most survivors are now painted in a grey overall finish.

Although designed as a long-range missile-armed interceptor, this big and heavy aircraft had enough agility to be the most important Western fighter of the 1960s and 1970s. It played a major part in the Vietnam, Yom Kippur and Iraq/Iran wars.

Some 5,195 F-4s had been delivered when the production line finally closed but this big fighter seems destined to serve well into the next century. Any air force planning to retire its fleet will have no difficulty finding would-be buyers.

The aircraft is an obvious candidate for midlife upgrading. Japan is retrofitting the APG-66 radar from the F-16, while Germany has chosen the APG-65 from the F/A-18.

Easily the most extensive rebuild is Israel's Phantom 2000. Starting in 1989, Israeli Air Force F-4s are being structurally strengthened to extend airframe life into the next century, as well as fully rewired electrically and given a new avionics suite based on the Elbit ACE-3 data processor. Modified aircraft receive a Norden/UTC multi-mode high-resolution radar, Elop wide-angle HUD, computerised weapon-delivery and navigation system, improved EW systems and a hands-on-throttle-and-stick(HOTAS) cockpit.

Flight tests in 1986-87 assessed the PW1120 turbofan as a replacement for the J79 engines. This resulted in lower weight, reduced fuel consumption, plus better manoeuvrability and climb rate, but was rejected on cost grounds.

McDONNELL DOUGLAS F-15 EAGLE

SPECIFICATION: F-15C Eagle.
Role: Air-superiority fighter.
Length: 63ft 9in (19.43m).
Height: 18ft 5.5in (5.63m).
Wingspan: 42ft 9.75in (13.05m).
Weights: Empty, 28,600lb (12,970kg);
loaded, 44,630lb (20,240kg); max. takeoff,
68,000lb (30,845kg).
Powerplant(s): Two Pratt & Whitney F100-
PW-100 turbofans.
Rating: 23,830lb (10,810kg) in afterburner.
Tactical radius: Not known.
Max. range: More than 2,500nm (4,631km)
with external tanks.
Max. speed: Greater than Mach 2.5.
Ceiling: 60,000ft (18,300m).
Armament: AIM-7 Sparrow and AIM-9
Sidewinder missiles, plus one 20mm Vulcan
M61 cannon.

Originally conceived in the late 1960s as a Mach 3 super-fighter able to match the performance of the MiG-25, the F-15 finally emerged as a Mach 2.3 aircraft with high manoeuvrability, a long-range radar and beyond-visual-range (BVR) missile armament. It flew for the first time in July 1972 and became operational in 1976.

Although similar in size to the F-4 Phantom it was intended to replace, it carried a much higher price tag. The USAF could afford such a warplane, but the only overseas customers for such a costly fighter were Israel, which receives massive US military aid, and oil-rich Saudi Arabia. Overall, in many

aerial battles, Israeli Eagles have downed more than 50 enemy fighters at no cost to themselves.

Two features give the F-15 its high performance – a wing large enough to ensure a low wing loading (a parameter often related to manoeuvrability) and twin turbofan engines with a high thrust-to-weight ratio. At typical combat weight, the F-15 is 10 per cent lighter than the F-4, but has almost a third more thrust.

Little could go wrong with the huge – and by modern standards simple – wing and the aircraft's advanced APG-63 radar proved trouble-free, but Pratt & Whitney's F100 engine pushed turbofan technology to its contemporary limits. In the early years of its service life, the aircraft was often dogged by engine problems.

Initial service versions were the F-15A single-seater and F-15B two-seater. These were followed in 1979 by the enhanced F-15C and F-15D versions, which have an improved radar and the ability to carry conformal fuel tanks – low-drag blister tanks which are mounted flush against the sides of the fuselage, adjacent to the air intakes.

The latest version to enter service is the F-15E, a two-seat aircraft able to carry out fighter and strike tasks. This carries a complex avionics suite which includes an APG-70 high-resolution radar with Doppler beam sharpening air-to-ground modes, an updated EW system, the LANTIRN day/night nav/attack system, a wide-angle HUD, plus multi-function cockpit displays. It's a complex system which requires a highly-trained crew.

Below: Although this Eagle was built more than 10 years ago, the skill of the USAF's ground crews will keep it combat-effective in the mid-1990s.

Above: When the West's "hottest" fighter goes hunting for an obsolete turboprop Soviet Bear bomber, there's nothing the latter can do to avoid being intercepted.

McDONNELL DOUGLAS F/A-18 HORNET

When the F/A-18 Hornet entered service in 1982, it set new standards in both combat versatility and cockpit effectiveness. Although larger and more expensive than the widely-exported F-16, it has won orders from Australia, Canada, South Korea, Kuwait, Spain and Switzerland.

On fighter missions, the basic Hornet can carry Sidewinder and Sparrow missiles. Its APG-65 multi-mode radar can track up to ten targets simultaneously, displaying data on up to eight at any one time.

Claims of multi-role capability are nothing new, but Hornet has been designed in such a way that the switch from fighter to attack roles is a matter of fitting the appropriate weapons, clipping on or removing attack sensors such as FLIR and laser-designation pods and adjusting the avionics software. The aircraft fully deserves its "F/A" designation.

Initial models were the F/A-18A and F/A-18B single and two-seaters. These were followed from 1987 onwards by the F/A-18C and F/A-18D, with superior computer and EW systems, an improved ejector seat and the ability to use new missiles like the AIM-120 AMRAAM and infra-red-guided versions of the AGM-65 Maverick.

The first Hornet with night-attack capability was an F-18D flown for the first time in May 1988. By 1990, all Hornets built for the US Navy/USMC were being delivered with the night-attack hardware. The new capability is provided by two more items of avionics, an advanced FLIR and a Thermal-Imaging Navigation Set (TINS).

A new specialised variant is the RF-18D, a two-seater which carries electro-optical and infra-red sensors in a nose bay, plus a sideways-looking radar in a pod on the fuselage centre-

Left: As the "F/A" designation suggests, the Hornet can dogfight or tote bombs as dictated by circumstances. Its electronics were designed with both roles in mind.

Below: The US Marine Corps was enthusiastic about the Hornet from the outset, for its ability to switch roles is ideal for amphibious operations.

> **SPECIFICATION:** F/A-18A Hornet.
> **Role:** Naval strike fighter.
> **Length:** 56ft 0in (17.07m).
> **Height:** 15ft 3.5in (4.66m).
> **Wingspan:** 37ft 6in (11.43m).
> **Weights:** Empty, 23,050lb (10,455kg); loaded, 36,710lb (16,650kg); max. takeoff, 49,200lb (22,320kg).
> **Powerplant(s):** Two General Electric F404-GE-400 turbofans.
> **Rating:** Approx. 16,000lb (7,260kg) in full afterburner.
> **Tactical radius:** Over 400nm (740km).
> **Max. range:** More than 2,000nm (3,700km).
> **Max. speed:** More than Mach 1.8.
> **Ceiling:** c.50,000ft (15,240m).
> **Armament:** AIM-7 and AIM-9 missiles, one 20mm cannon and 17,000lb (7,700kg) of ordnance.

line. Imagery from these sensors can be transmitted to the ground in real time via a datalink.

Current F404 engines deliver around 16,000lb (7,257kg) of thrust, but General Electric is offering the 17,700lb (8,029kg) F404-GE-402 Enhanced Performance Engine for Hornets built from 1992 onwards.

For the mid to late 1990s, McDonnell Douglas has proposed the Hornet 2000. This is not a single design, but seven options which range from a simple avionics upgrade of the current aircraft to a heavily-modified design with a cranked delta wing, canards and manoeuvrability-enhancing CCV technology. Intermediate options include various combinations of features such as a stretched fuselage, larger wings, additional internal fuel and even more powerful engines.

McDONNELL DOUGLAS A-4 SKYHAWK

References to "pilot's airplanes" and "classic warplanes" usually mean fighters, but no-one could deny these accolades to the A-4 Skyhawk. In conceiving the aircraft back in 1952, Ed Heinemann of what was then Douglas Aircraft set himself to design a small bomber of about half the weight which the US Navy expected, while offering an extra 100kts (185km/hr) in speed and an extra 100 miles (160km) in tactical radius.

The USN probably thought that one of its favourite designers was suffering from delusions of grandeur, but Heinemann was right. It could be done, and his team did it, creating an aircraft which remained in production for a quarter of a century.

In its original A4D-1 form (later redesignated A-4A), Skyhawk was a simple aircraft with minimal avionics, driven by a 7,700lb (3,493kg) thrust Curtiss Wright J65 turbojet and with a maximum takeoff weight of around 22,500lb (10,206kg). The A-4M being delivered in the late 1970s weighed up to 27,420lb (12,437kg) at takeoff, was powered by an 11,200lb (5,080kg) Pratt & Whitney J52 engine and needed a dorsal bulge to house a range of

SPECIFICATION: A-4M Skyhawk.
Role: Strike fighter.
Length: 40ft 3.2in (12.27m).
Height: 15ft 0in (4.57m).
Wingspan: 27ft 6in (8.38m).
Weights: Empty, 10,465lb (4,747kg); max. takeoff, 27,420lb (12,437kg).
Powerplant(s): One Pratt & Whitney J52-P-8A turbojet.
Rating: 11,200lb (5,080kg).
Tactical radius: 290nm (538km) with 4,000lb (1,814kg) ordnance load.
Max. range: 1,785nm (3,307km).
Max. speed: 582kts (1,078km/hr) at low level; Mach 0.94 at altitude.
Ceiling: c.49,000ft (14,900m).
Armament: Up to 8,200lb (3,720kg) of ordnance, plus two 20mm Mk12 cannon.

Above: US Navy and Marine Corps pilots polish their deck-landing technique in the two-seat TA-4J trainer.

modern avionics including terrain-following radar, digital weapon-delivery computer and inertial navigation kit.

The Skyhawk's qualities resulted in major sales to eight export customers. With the US fleet now all but retired and Israel's mostly in storage, the sheer number of second-hand aircraft potentially available will no doubt greatly hamper efforts to market the Italian/Brazilian AMX.

The aircraft is a "natural" for retrofit schemes. New Zealand is modifying its Skyhawks with an avionics suite based on that of the F-16, while Singapore has replaced the J65 with an unreheated F404 turbofan.

Below: This New Zealand A-4K is fitted with the avionics "hump" that was first seen on Skyhawks supplied to the Israelis.

McDONNELL DOUGLAS/BAe AV-8B/HARRIER GR.5

Development of this second-generation member of the Harrier family was begun in the USA by McDonnell Douglas during the late 1970s and it met with stiff Congressional opposition along the way before deliveries started in January 1984. The type became operational with the Marines during August 1985 and the service hopes to buy 304. The trainer version is the two-seat TAV-8B which first flew on 21 October 1986.

The engine used for initial deliveries was the 21,450lb (9,730kg) thrust F402-RR-406A Pegasus II but later aircraft have the 23,800lb (10,795kg) F402-RR-408 Pegasus 11-61.

In RAF service, it is known as the Harrier GR.5 and a British-built aircraft got airborne on 30 April 1985. Two development machines paved the way for 60 production examples and these began to join the RAF in July 1987 but the GR.5 was not to become operational until mid-1989. By 1991, three squadrons will be using the new Harrier, including two in Germany.

At first, the RAF hoped to train crews on Harrier T.4 two-seaters used to convert pilots to the older Harrier GR.3, but it now plans to buy the two-seat TAV-8B as the T.10 version.

Harrier II aircraft manufactured in Britain for service in the Royal Air Force utilise a slightly different version of the Pegasus turbofan. Known as the Mk.105, maximum power output is 21,750lb (9,865kg).

Above: Continual updating has permitted the AV-8B to take on new roles. One recent addition has expanded its capability and it is now able to operate by night.

> **SPECIFICATION:** AV-8B/Harrier GR.5
> **Role:** V/STOL close-support aircraft.
> **Length:** 46ft 4in (14.12m).
> **Height:** 11ft 7.75in (3.55m).
> **Wingspan:** 30ft 4in (9.25m).
> **Weights:** Empty, 13,086lb (5,936kg); loaded, 22,950lb (10,410kg); max. takeoff, 31,000lb (14,060kg).
> **Powerplant(s):** One Rolls-Royce F402-RR-406 Pegasus 11-21 turbofan.
> **Rating:** 21,750lb (9,865kg).
> **Tactical radius:** 90-480nm (167-889km) depending on weapon load.
> **Max. range:** 2,120nm (3,929km) with external fuel.
> **Max. speed:** Mach 0.85 at sea level, Mach 0.91 at altitude.
> **Armament:** 9,200lb (4,170kg) of ordnance, plus gun pack with one 25mm cannon.

Below: The AV-8B is basically a bomb carrier for support of USMC amphibious operations.

Modern armies can fight by night, so close support must be available around the clock. On 26 June 1987, McDonnell Douglas flew the first AV-8B with night attack capability. New avionics mostly come from the UK and include a GEC Sensors FLIR and Smiths Industries colour head-down cockpit displays plus a wide-angle HUD. In its latest form, it also has a Honeywell colour digital moving map system while pilots must wear night-vision goggles.

The RAF night-attack version is the Harrier GR.7 Nightbird, 34 being ordered in 1988. Existing GR.5s will be updated to GR.7 standard which is similar to the US version but uses a GEC Sensors digital colour map unit.

The sole export customer so far is Spain, but Italy's new carrier *Giuseppe Garibaldi* will need V/STOL aircraft in the early 1990s.

MIKOYAN MiG-21 FISHBED & XIAN J-7

This small fighter has been built in greater numbers and in more variants than any other supersonic warplane. The original version entered Soviet Air Force service in 1959, and in developed form it remained in production in the Soviet Union until as recently as the late 1980s.

The first generation MiG-21F day fighter models were powered by the 12,676lb (5,750kg) thrust Tumansky R-11 two-spool turbojet, as were early all-weather versions such as the MiG-21PF, FL, PFM and PFMA.

The latter version, known to NATO as "Fishbed-J", was the first multi-role model, able to fly strike and intercept missions. Re-engined with the more powerful 14,550lb (6,600kg) R-13 turbojet in 1970, it became the first of a new series which included the hump-backed SMT interceptor and the first model of MiG-21bis.

In the 1980s, the MiG-21bis was re-engined with the R-25 turbojet. For several years, Western observers ar-gued whether the thrust in full after-burner was 17,637lb or 19,840lb, figures which correspond to 8,000 kg and 9,000 kg respectively, before generally settling for more modest values of around 16,500lb (7,484 kg). Some East European sources have sug-gested higher power ratings for this engine, but these seem unlikely.

China builds its own version of the MiG-21. Powered by the Wopen 7, an unlicensed copy of the R-11, this is known as the J-7. Pakistan operates the F-7M Skybolt, an export version fitted with four underwing hardpoints, while the F-7MP flight tested in 1988 has an improved cockpit with Collins navigation avionics.

Development of the J-7/F-7 has been hampered by the low thrust of the Wopen 7. SNECMA is now collaborat-ing with the Liyang Engine Company to develop the improved WP-13G and WP-14 engines for use on advanced F-7 models. The new F-7 III is reportedly similar to the MiG-21MF. Probably fit-ted with Western avionics, it may have entered production in 1986-87.

The Soviet Union is now offering ex-port customers a new light fighter based on the MiG-21bis airframe and powered by the Isotov RD-33 turbofan used in the MiG-29. This aircraft may be designated MiG-35.

SPECIFICATION: MiG-21MF "Fishbed-J"
Role: Multi-role fighter.
Length: 51ft 8.5in (15.76m).
Height: 14ft 9in (4.5m).
Wingspan: 23ft 5.5in (7.15m).
Weights: Empty, 12,500lb (5,700kg); loaded, 18,100lb (8,200kg); max. takeoff, 21,600lb (9,800kg).
Powerplant(s): One Tumansky R-13-300 turbojet.
Rating: 14,550lb (6,600kg) in afterburner.
Tactical radius: 400nm (740km) with one ton of bombs plus external fuel.
Max. range: 590nm (1,100km).
Max. speed: Mach 2.1 at altitude.
Ceiling: c.50,000ft (15,200m).
Armament: One 23mm GSh-23 cannon, plus AA-2 "Atoll" missiles or one ton of ordnance.

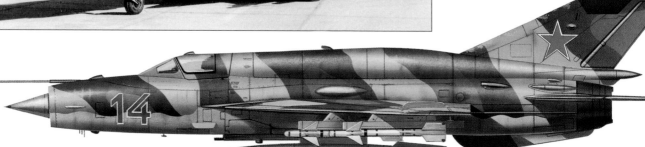

Left: Clever redesign work in the mid-1970s resulted in the MiG-21bis, an improved model which introduced the new higher-thrust R-25 engine and far superior avionics.

Below: The hump-backed MiG-21SMT packed a heavy fuel load into its fuselage tanks, but few were built.

MIKOYAN MiG-23 & MiG-27 FLOGGER

Designed in the early 1960s as a medium-weight fighter able to handle the air-superiority and strike roles, the MiG-23 was the first Soviet warplane to use variable-geometry in order to reduce takeoff and landing speeds. Empty weight is about twice that of the MiG-21, allowing the MiG-23 to carry a powerful J-band "High Lark" long-range radar, a heavy weapon load, plus enough fuel for a good radius of action.

Acceleration is good, but the aircraft lacks the fine handling qualities of the older MiG-21. Its combat record has been dismal — the Syrians lost 36 in combat during the 1982 Israeli invasion of Lebanon.

The first model fielded in quantity was the MiG-23M fighter, which entered service with the Soviet Air Force in 1972. This was powered by a single Tumansky R-27 turbojet, a unit which developed 22,487lb (10,200kg) of thrust with afterburning and water-injection, but it was soon followed by the MiG-23MF fitted with the 27,558lb (12,500kg) R-29B engine.

The MiG-23ML first seen in the late 1970s has a smaller vertical fin and often carries an undernose sensor pod. It was further developed into an improved version known to NATO as "Flogger-K". Aircraft now being delivered to the Soviet Air Force use an improved engine known as the R-29PN. The MiG-23MS is an export model fitted with simpler avionics, including the "Jay Bird" radar as used on late-model MiG-21s.

In 1971 a dedicated strike derivative was fielded. Known as the MiG-27, this has a redesigned forward fuselage, whose steeply-sloped nose contains no radar but is fitted with a laser range-finder. The cockpit is armoured and the inlets have been redesigned into a simpler pattern suited to low-level slower-speed operations. These feed a single R-29-300 engine with a smaller afterburner and a short two-position exhaust nozzle, offering 25,350lb (11,499kg) maximum thrust.

Another attack version probably developed at the request of export users is the MiG-23BN. This combines the strike-configured forward fuselage of the MiG-27 with the inlets, aft fuselage and powerplant that are installed on the normal MiG-23 fighter.

SPECIFICATION: MiG-23MF "Flogger-B"
Role: Air superiority/strike fighter.
Length: 55ft 1.5in (16.80m).
Height: 14ft 4in (4.35m).
Wingspan: 26ft 9in (8.17m) swept; 46ft 9in (14.25m) unswept.
Weights: Empty, 24,250lb (11,000kg); loaded, 34,390lb (15,600kg); max. takeoff, 44,300lb (20,100kg).
Powerplant(s): One Tumansky R-29B turbojet.
Rating: 17,600lb (8,000kg) dry thrust, 27,500lb (12,500kg) with afterburning.
Tactical radius: 485-700nm (900-1,300km).
Max. speed: Mach 2.35.
Ceiling: 61,000ft (18,600m).
Armament: One 23mm GSh-23 cannon plus four AA-8 "Aphid" and two AA-7 "Apex" missiles.

Right: The large nose radome on MiG-23s used by the Soviet Union and the Warsaw Pact hides a "High Lark" radar, a unit not cleared for general export.

Below: The smaller radome on this Libyan Air Force MiG-23MF houses a version of the "Jay Bird" radar of late model MiG-21s.

MIKOYAN MiG-25 FOXBAT & MiG-31 FOXHOUND

The MiG-25 "Foxbat" was developed to meet the threat posed by the USAF's planned B-70 Mach 3 bomber, but even before the "Foxbat" prototype flew in 1964, plans to deploy the B-70 had been abandoned. Given the existence of Lockheed's A-12 and its SR-71 derivative, the Soviets pressed on with this huge Mach 2.8 fighter. To cut cost and ease development problems, steel rather than titanium was used for the structure, while the Tumansky R-26 turbojet was adapted from the engine originally conceived for use by the Yastreb Mach 3 reconnaissance drone.

Development was protracted and the aircraft did not attain squadron service until 1970. With "Foxbat", the Soviet Union had effectively shot itself in the foot. The aircraft and its massive AA-6 "Acrid" air-to-air missiles lacked the performance to cope with the Lockheed SR-71 Blackbird, while its reputed Mach 3 capability spurred development of the F-15.

The improved MiG-25M fielded in the 1980s has an uprated engine and an improved radar, but the most militarily useful variants are probably the MiG-25R reconnaissance aircraft and a specialised anti-radar version fielded in the late 1980s. In NATO parlance, the latter is known as "Foxbat-F".

Below: Space was found within the MiG-31's bulky fuselage for a second cockpit to house a weapon system operator tasked with managing the radar and long-range AA-9 missiles.

Above: High-speed and high-altitude photo-reconnaissance missions are undertaken by the camera-equipped MiG-25R "Foxbat-B" which has a different nose configuration.

By 1981, the Soviet Air Force was taking delivery of the MiG-31 "Foxhound". This has a stretched fuselage with a rear cockpit for a radar operator. "Foxhound" retains the steel structure of the MiG-25, but has a lower top speed estimated at around Mach 2.4.

The R-26 turbojet engine used in "Foxbat" was optimised for high-speed dash performance, so was replaced on the "Foxhound" by the Tumansky R-31F turbofan. This is thought to develop 30,865lb (14,000kg) with afterburning. "Foxhound" carries long-range AA-9 "Amos" missiles which combine the range of the older AA-6 "Acrid" with modern snap-up/snap-down guidance.

SPECIFICATION: MiG-31 "Foxhound"
Role: Interceptor.
Length: 70ft 6.5in (21.5m).
Height: 18ft 6in (5.63m).
Wingspan: 45ft 11in (14.0m).
Weights: Empty, 48,000lb (21,800kg); loaded, 85,000lb (38,500kg); max. takeoff, 90,000lb (41,000kg).
Powerplant(s): Two Tumansky R-31F turbofans.
Rating: 30,865lb (14,000kg) with afterburning.
Tactical radius: 800nm (1,480km).
Max. range: Not known.
Max. speed: Mach 2.4.
Ceiling: 75,000ft (23,000m).
Armament: Four AA-9 air-to-air missiles.

MIKOYAN MiG-29 FULCRUM

Above: The MiG-29 cannot be described as an attractive aircraft but widely-spaced engines plus the tail fins and wing leading edge extensions are all excellent features.

Like the F-4 Phantom, the MiG-29 is one of those aircraft which looks utterly wrong, yet its aerodynamic performance comes close to matching that of the best Western fighters of its generation. A great weakness of earlier types such as the MiG-19 and MiG-21 was their small size, but with the MiG-29 the Mikoyan team moved to an aircraft with size and weight characteristics in the class of the F/A-18 Hornet rather than the F-16 Fighting Falcon.

SPECIFICATION: MiG-29 "Fulcrum-A"
Role: Air-superiority fighter.
Length: 56ft 10in (17.32m).
Height: 15ft 3in (4.73m).
Wingspan: 37ft 3in (11.36m).
Weights: Empty, 18,025lb (8,175kg); loaded, c.33,000lb (15,000kg); max. takeoff, c.39,700lb (18,000kg).
Powerplant(s): Two Isotov RD-33 low bypass ratio turbofans.
Rating: 11,240lb (5,098kg) dry thrust, 18,300lb (8,300kg) with afterburning.
Tactical radius: 383nm (710km).
Max. range: c.1,130nm (2,100km) with external fuel.
Max. speed: Greater than Mach 2.3.
Ceiling: 55,700ft (17,000m).
Armament: AA-10 "Alamo" and AA-11 "Archer" missiles, plus one 30mm cannon.

Below: The high cockpit and curved canopy are better than those of the MiG-21 or MiG-23 but are still inferior to those on US aircraft such as the F-15 and F-16.

Another break from tradition was to get the engine not from the Tumansky bureau but from Isotov, an organisation better known for its helicopter powerplants. Despite their inexperience in the fighter field, this design office created an engine which comes close to matching the performance of the General Electric F404.

Visibility from the cockpit of late-model MiG-21s was poor, but the canopy of the MiG-29 is the classic fighter type, although smaller than those on current US fighters.

The technology in the nose-mounted pulse-Doppler radar is probably similar to that of the radar in the F-16, but the Soviet fighter also has an electro-optical tracker which incorporates a laser ranger.

One novel but clever feature is the use of retractable doors to close the intakes while the aircraft nosewheel is on the ground. These prevent slush or loose material from entering the inlet during the takeoff and landing run. While the inlet is closed, the engines draw air from a series of doors in the upper surface.

The MiG-29 can carry the latest generation of agile air-to-air missiles such as the AA-10 and AA-11 and also has a 30mm cannon which is located in the port wing root.

An improved version with fly-by-wire controls and a CRT-based cockpit is presently under development. If all goes well, this model could enter service in the mid-1990s.

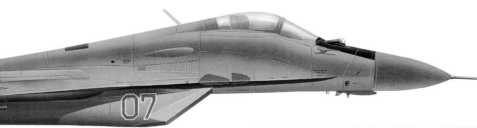

MITSUBISHI F-1

Combat aircraft are often developed into trainers, but Mitsubishi's F-1 is a rare example of the opposite process – a fighter developed from a trainer. Designed in the late 1960s and flown for the first time in July 1971, the T-2A trainer was an aircraft in the performance class of SEPECAT's Jaguar. It even shared the same general configuration and powerplant.

From the beginning of the project, an FS-T2kai strike version was envisaged. It would be a relatively easy modification, with avionics being packed into what had been the rear cockpit and the rear canopy replaced by a metal fairing. The avionics suite is based on a nose-mounted Mitsubishi AWG-12 radar, a Ferranti inertial nav/attack system, an ASQ-1 weapon-aiming computer, a Thomson-CSF HUD and an APR-3 radar-warning receiver.

The first example flew in July 1975, six months after the first production T-2A. Deliveries started in 1977 and the F-1 gradually replaced the obsolete F-86F Sabres previously used for ground attack. Some 77 were built for the JASDF, but no attempt was made to export the aircraft – Japan does not export weaponry of any type – so the line closed in 1987.

At first the aircraft carried bombs or unguided rockets on its four underwing hardpoints, the inboard locations also being plumbed for fuel tanks. Another plumbed hardpoint is on the fuselage centreline and the aircraft is fitted with a single internally-mounted M61A1 20mm cannon.

Above: The Mitsubishi F-1 is visually similar to the SEPECAT Jaguar and is powered by a licence-built version of the same Adour turbofan engine.

The early 1980s saw the introduction of the Mitsubishi ASM-1 anti-ship missile, a rocket-powered weapon with a radar seeker and a range of up to 31 miles (50km). This modification required a new fire-control computer. Development of a longer-ranged variant of the ASM-1 powered by a jet engine was then begun.

Under present plans, the F-1 will serve until the mid-1990s when it will be replaced by the new FS-X, a canard-equipped derivative of the F-16. In the meantime, the F-1 is the subject of a life-extension programme.

The engines used are licence-built Adour 102s rated at only 7,305lb (3,313kg) thrust, so by the standards of the RAF Jaguar, the Mitsubishi F-1 is somewhat underpowered.

SPECIFICATION: F-1
Role: Strike fighter.
Length: 56ft 9.5in (17.31m).
Height: 14ft 4.25in (4.38m).
Wingspan: 25ft 10.25in (7.88m).
Weights: Empty, 14,017lb (6,358kg); max. takeoff, 30,146lb (13,674kg).
Powerplant(s): Two licence-built Rolls-Royce/Turbomeca Adour turbofans.
Rating: 4,710lb (2,136kg) dry; 7,070lb (3,207kg) with afterburning.
Tactical radius: 300nm (556km) hi-lo-hi.
Max. range: c.1,400nm (2,600km).
Max. speed: Mach 1.6 at altitude.
Ceiling: 50,000ft (15,240m).
Armament: 6,000lb (2,720kg) of ordnance, plus one JM61 20mm cannon.

Below: The noticeable bulge behind the F-1's cockpit contains avionics equipment required by the strike mission.

NAMC Q-5/A-5

When reports of a Chinese-developed MiG-19 variant fitted with side inlets first reached the West in the 1970s, it was assumed to be a radar-equipped interceptor. In reality, the end product turned out to be the Q-5, a strike aircraft complete with a miniature internal weapons bay.

The modifications needed to turn the basic J-6 (MiG-19) into a side-inlet fighter-bomber were not simply a matter of splicing on a new nose. A longer fuselage allowed internal fuel capacity to be increased by 70 per cent, the wing was increased in span to maintain the wing loading, the fuselage spine was reconfigured to match the revised cockpit and canopy and the undercarriage was strengthened to cope with the increased weight. Powerplant was the Shenyang Wopen 6 turbojet, derived from Tumansky's RD-9BF-81.

Above: The weapon pylons of the A-5 are lightly stressed, minimising the weapon load.

SPECIFICATION: Q-5 (A-5) "Fantan"
Role: Ground-attack aircraft.
Length: 51ft 4.1in (15.65m).
Height: 14ft 9.5in (4.51m).
Wingspan: 31ft 10in (9.70m).
Weights: Empty, 14,317lb (6,494kg); loaded, 21,010lb (9,530kg); Max. takeoff, 26,455lb (12,000kg).
Powerplant(s): Two Wopen 6 afterburning turbojets.
Rating: 5,732lb (2,600kg) dry; 7,165lb (3,250kg) with afterburning.
Tactical radius: 324nm (600km) hi-lo-hi.
Max. range: c.1,080nm (2,000km).
Max. speed: 653kts (1,210km/hr) at sea level; Mach 1.12 at altitude.
Ceiling: 52,500ft (16,000m).
Armament: 4,410lb (2,000kg) of ordnance plus two 23mm cannon.

The improved A-5K developed in the late 1980s seems to have been intended for use by the Chinese Air Force. This had a French avionics suite which included a Thomson-CSF HUD and laser rangefinder, a Sagem INS and a TRT radar altimeter. However, in the early summer of 1990, work on this version was abandoned.

The A-5M is intended as an export model. Developed with Italian assistance, this has an avionics suite based on that of the AMX, including a ranging radar, radar-warning receiver, two digital computers and a dual-redundant databus. Other changes include two more hardpoints under the outer wings and the uprated Wopen 6A engine. This has variable inlet stators, a redesigned first-stage compressor, a revised hot section and a new afterburner. These modifications to the aircraft added 309lb (140kg) to its empty weight. The first prototype flew on 30 August 1988, but was written off when it crashed two months later. Flight testing was later resumed using a second modified aircraft.

Below: Pakistan's Air Force was the first export customer for the simple but rugged A-5 fighter-bomber.

NORTHROP F-5

The original single-seat F-5A and two-seater F-5B were, by the standards of contemporary supersonic fighters, relatively simple and inexpensive aircraft. Able to cope with the threat posed by the MiG-17 or MiG-19, the F-5A lacked the range and payload-carrying capability to pose a threat in the strike role. It was thus an ideal aircraft for supply to air arms of friendly non-NATO countries.

The F-5 even proved attractive to some NATO countries, with Canada, Denmark, Greece, Netherlands, Norway, Spain and Turkey all operating the type. More than 1,000 were built in a production run which ended in 1971. This included licence manufacture in Canada as the CF-5 and NF-5.

By this time, the F-5A/B was outclassed by the MiG-21, so the US Department of Defense held a competition to select a design for a new International Fighter. This was won by Northrop's F-5E, a revised design with more internal fuel, manoeuvrability-enhancing wing leading-edge root extensions and improved J85-GE-21A turbojet engines.

The F-5E and its F-5F two-seat counterpart were much more potent aircraft than their predecessors. Both

carried a radar and could tote a much heavier ordnance load. The F-5E's first flight came during August 1972, allowing deliveries to overseas customers to begin a year later.

Small and agile, the F-5E proved a tricky air-combat opponent and was selected by the USAF and US Navy to equip their "Aggressor" training units. Like the F-5A, it was also available in a dedicated reconnaissance version.

A production run of around 325 had originally been envisaged by the US DoD, but the final total was roughly 1,400 for more than 30 customers. Most aircraft were built by Northrop, but licence-production also took place in South Korea, Switzerland and Taiwan. The US production line closed in 1987, but enough major assemblies were in stock to allow small batches to be delivered in 1988 and 1989.

Below: Switzerland was the last overseas air arm to buy the hugely successful Tiger II in bulk and also received a small number of F-5F two-seaters for training tasks.

In 1982 Northrop flew the first prototype of a single-engined version. Powered by a 17,000lb (7,711kg) thrust General Electric F404, this was known as the F-20 Tigershark. Two of the three examples that were built were destroyed on demonstration flights and the project was abandoned before the fourth had flown.

SPECIFICATION: F-5E Tiger II.
Role: Light tactical fighter.
Length: 47ft 5in (14.45m).
Height: 13ft 4in (4.07m).
Wingspan: 26ft 8in (8.13m).
Weights: Empty, 9,723lb (4,410kg); max. takeoff, 24,772lb (11,214kg).
Powerplant(s): Two General Electric J85-GE-21B turbojets.
Rating: 5,000lb (2,268kg) with afterburning.
Tactical radius: Typically 480-570nm (890-1,056km).
Max. range: 1,545nm (2,863km) with external tanks.
Max. speed: Mach 1.64 at altitude.
Ceiling: 51,800ft (15,790m).
Armament: Up to 7,000lb (3,175kg) of ordnance plus two 20mm M39A2 cannon.

Below: Jordan is a long-established Middle Eastern F-5 user and has operated most models. This is an F-5E.

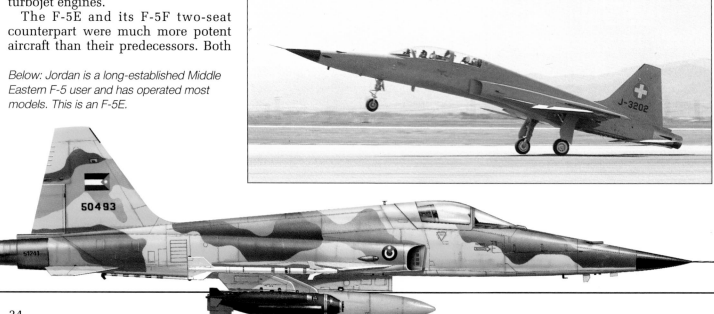

PANAVIA TORNADO IDS & ADV

Developed in the late 1960s and early 1970s by Germany, Italy and the UK, this potent warplane has been fielded in three basic versions. All major assemblies are built by only one nation, but each country set up a national production line.

All three nations operate the basic Interdictor Strike (IDS) model, a strike

SPECIFICATION: Tornado IDS.
Role: Multi-role combat aircraft.
Length: 54ft 10.25in (16.72m).
Height: 19ft 6.25in (5.95m).
Wingspan: 28 ft 2.5in (8.60m) swept; 45ft 7.5in (13.91m) unswept.
Weights: Empty, 31,065lb (14,091kg); loaded, 45,000lb (20,410kg); max. takeoff, c.60,000lb (27,200kg).
Powerplant(s): Two Turbo-Union RB.199 Mk.103 turbofans.
Rating: 16,920lb (7,675kg) in afterburner.
Tactical radius: 750nm (1,390km) hi-lo-hi with heavy weapons load.
Max. range: c.2,100nm (3,890km).
Max. speed: Mach 2.2 clean, Mach 0.92 with external stores.
Armament: 18,000lb (8,165kg) of ordnance plus two 27mm Mauser cannon.

aircraft not much bigger than an F-16, whose ordnance load rivals that of the F-4 or Su-24, but which can be carried for a longer range and with a dramatically lower fuel burn thanks to the RB.199 Mk.103 engines.

The UK is the only one of the three Panavia member states to operate the Air Defence Variant (ADV). This has a stretched fuselage, uprated Mk.104 engines and an avionics suite based on the GEC Avionics Foxhunter radar. The first F.2 production model had the earlier Mk.103 engine and lacked the automatic wing sweep and automatic flap/slat scheduling system introduced by the definitive F.3 aircraft. When retrofitted with the F.3 sweep and slat/flap systems, the F.2 will be redesignated as the F.2A.

Problems with radar had not been ironed out by the time the set had to

Below: Skyflash and Sidewinder missiles are visible in this fine head-on study of an RAF Tornado F.3 as it goes about its combat air patrol task somewhere over the North Sea.

enter production, so some aircraft were delivered with sub-standard radars or, in some cases, no radar at all. The problem was due in part to an upgrading of the radar specification, but a multi-stage ''get-well'' programme to improve the situation is under way.

The final version is the Tornado Electronic Combat Reconnaissance (ECR) model operated only by West Germany, although a small Italian order is expected. Based on the IDS, this carries an emitter-location system, low/medium altitude reconnaissance sensors, a data link and underwing jamming pods. The UK has the GR.1A for reconnaissance, this essentially being a GR.1 modified to carry internally-mounted IR sensors.

Export sales have been poor. Saudi Arabia operates 48 IDS and 24 ADV aircraft bought in the mid-eighties, but small orders from Oman, Jordan and Malaysia proved short-lived. A Saudi follow-on order also looks vulnerable to cancellation and some RAF aircraft have recently been axed.

Below: West Germany's Marineflieger uses the Tornado IDS aircraft to police the waters of the Baltic. In the maritime role, the primary weapon is the Kormoran anti-ship missile.

SAAB-SCANIA 37 VIGGEN

As the final pages of this book were being written in July 1990, a press release from Saab-Scania announced delivery of the 329th and final Viggen fighter – a JA37 interceptor. This marked the end of a well-conceived programme started almost three decades earlier. Total deliveries fell well short of the 500 plus predicted in the project's early days, but Viggen remains an impressive testimony to the aviation skills of a nation of only eight million people.

The concept was a bold one – to develop a single multi-role aircraft able to combine the strike power of the F-105 Thunderchief with the interceptor capability of the F-106 Delta Dart, but adding reconnaissance and anti-ship capability for good measure. In retrospect, it still seems amazing that the concept worked so well. Not only did the design use a locally-developed engine - the most powerful afterburning turbofan of its day – but it also featured a canard layout. Common in present-day designs, this seemed more akin to science-fiction when it appeared in the early 1960s.

Development of the engine was tackled by Volvo Flygmotor, which took the well-proven Pratt & Whitney

SPECIFICATION: JA37 Viggen.
Role: Interceptor.
Length: 51ft 1.5in (15.60m).
Height: 19ft 4.25in (5.90m).
Wingspan: 34ft 9.25in (10.60m).
Weights: Empty, not known; loaded, c.33,070lb (15,000kg); max. takeoff, c.37,500lb (17,000kg).
Powerplant(s): One Volvo Flygmotor RM8B turbofan.
Rating: 16,203lb (7,350kg) dry thrust; 28,108lb (12,750kg) with afterburning.
Tactical radius: 540nm+ (1,000km) hi-lo-hi; 270nm+ (500km) lo-lo-lo.
Max. range: Not known.
Max. speed: Mach 2+ at altitude; Mach 1.2 at 330ft (100m).
Armament: Skyflash and AIM-9 Sidewinder missiles, plus one 30mm KCA cannon.

Right: Lacking radar, the nose of the SF37 is packed with reconnaissance cameras.

JT8D civil turbofan, redesigned the compressor stages for supersonic flight and added an afterburner. The resulting RM8A engine developed 14,750lb (6,690kg) of dry thrust and 26,000lb (11,793kg) in afterburner.

The first prototype Viggen flew in 1967. A fleet of seven trials aircraft cleared the way for the entry into service in 1971 of the AJ37 attack Viggen equipped with the Ericsson UAP 1011 multi-mode radar.

Next version was the SK37 two-seat trainer, followed by the SF37 for reconnaissance with a camera-packed nose and there was also the radar-equipped SH37 derivative dedicated to maritime reconnaissance.

Development of the JA37 interceptor started in 1968, but the prototype did not fly until December 1975. For this aircraft, Volvo Flygmotor created the 28,108lb (12,750kg) thrust RM8B engine, while Ericsson developed the UAP-1023 pulse-Doppler radar. Long-range firepower was provided by BAe's Sky Flash missile. Development was protracted, with the JA37 finally becoming operational in 1980. All models of Viggen will remain in service until the deployment of the JAS39 Gripen in the mid-1990s.

Below: The AJ37 is the basic attack model of the Viggen and uses Ericsson PS37 radar plus the Volvo Flygmotor RM8A engine.

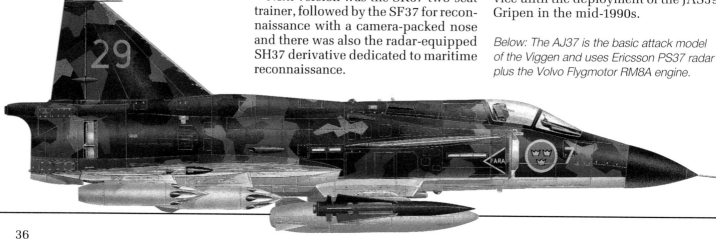

SAAB-SCANIA JAS39 GRIPEN

When an industrial consortium led by Saab-Scania responded to a 1980 decision by the Swedish Parliament to order the development of a Viggen replacement, they set out to design a canard delta multi-role fighter roughly half the weight of the existing aircraft. The resulting design, known as Jakt Attack Spaning, was evaluated in 1981-82 against foreign designs such as the F-16, F-18, the proposed F-18L de-navalised Hornet, the F-20 and the Mirage 2000, but in June 1982 the Swedish Parliament ordered development of the local design to begin.

Like Viggen, the new fighter (now named JAS39 Gripen) would have a Volvo Flygmotor engine based on a US design. The RM12 would be a derivative of the General Electric F404, but uprated to give 18,000lb (8,165kg) of thrust and strengthened for greater resistance to bird-strikes.

Other agreements provided technology needed for the new fighter. Extensive use would be made of composite materials and British Aerospace

> **SPECIFICATION:** JAS39 Gripen.
> **Role:** Multi-role fighter.
> **Length:** c.46ft (14m).
> **Height:** Not known.
> **Wingspan:** c.26ft (8m).
> **Weights:** Empty, not known; loaded, c.18,000lb (8,160kg); max. takeoff, not known.
> **Powerplant(s):** One Volvo Flygmotor RM12 turbofan.
> **Rating:** c.18,000lb (8,160kg) with afterburning.
> **Tactical radius:** Not known.
> **Max. range:** Not known.
> **Max. speed:** Mach 2 at altitude.
> **Ceiling:** Not known.
> **Armament:** Missiles, bombs, and one 27mm Mauser BK27 cannon.

was made chief sub-contractor for the wing. A deal between L. M. Ericsson and Ferranti covered technological assistance with the multi-mode PS-05A pulse-Doppler radar, while Honeywell Corporation would provide the laser inertial navigation system and Hughes the wide-angle head-up display unit.

Like the canard deltas taking shape during the mid-1980s in the UK, France and Israel, Gripen would have a digital fly-by-wire system. A FLIR system would be available in pod-mounted form, while the cockpit had three cathode-ray-tube displays.

Construction of the first of five prototypes started in 1984. Roll-out was in April 1987, but the maiden flight did not take place until 9 December 1988. It crashed on 2 February 1989 and the resulting investigation blamed the accident on problems with the software of the flight-control system. Finding a solution took time and flight testing was not resumed with the second prototype until the summer of 1990.

Deployment has slipped to 1993, but an eventual total of at least 140 is planned and may rise to 300. This will probably include between 20 and 30 two-seat JAS39B trainers.

Below: The short-lived first Gripen prototype was destroyed when it crashed due to problems with the flight control system.

Below: When it enters service with Sweden's Air Force, Gripen will carry payloads such as the BOZ chaff pod and the Saab-Scania RBS.15F anti-ship missile plus the heat-seeking AIM-9 Sidewinder for aerial combat.

SEPECAT JAGUAR

Initial production of this multi-role fighter was for the air forces of the UK and France, which took delivery of 203 and 200 respectively. France was evidently reluctant to promote the aircraft for export – it was too direct a competitor to the Mirage – so this task fell to the UK. Export efforts were focussed on Jaguar International, a standard similar to that used by the RAF, but with uprated engines. This started with the 8,040lb (3,647kg)

Below: Export customers have specified an avionics standard similar to that of the RAF. This aircraft is a British Jaguar GR.1.

thrust Adour Mk.804, but later received the 8,400lb (3,810kg) Mk.811.

The type attracted few buyers. By the time that Anglo-French production ended in the late 1980s, a further 94 had been built, made up of 12 for Ecuador, 24 for Oman, 18 for Nigeria and 40 for India.

Following this initial purchase for the Indian Air Force, Hindustan Aeronautics Ltd (HAL) began local assembly. The first of a further 45 assembled from European components flew in 1982, followed in 1988 by the first of 46 aircraft of local manufacture. Some Indian Jaguars were custom-built for the maritime strike role, being equipped with nose-mounted Thomson-CSF Agave radars, a Smiths Industries Darin nav/attack system and AM.39 Exocet anti-ship guided missiles.

RAF Jaguars have been retrofitted with the Adour Mk.104, similar in thrust to the Mk.804 engines used on early Jaguar Internationals and have received a Ferranti FIN 1064 INS system in place of the original GEC-Marconi NAVWASS. The Ferranti INS has also been fitted to Omani aircraft.

Below: The Sultan of Oman's Air Force has two squadrons with Sidewinder-armed Jaguar International strike fighters.

38

SHENYANG J-8 FINBACK

SPECIFICATION: F-8 "Finback"
Role: Interceptor.
Length: 70ft 10in (21.59m).
Height: 17ft 9in (5.41m).
Wingspan: 30ft 8in (9.34m).
Weights: Empty, 21,649lb (9,820kg); loaded, 31,526lb (14,300kg); max. takeoff, 39,242lb (17,800kg).
Powerplant(s): Two Wopen 13 afterburning turbojets.
Rating: 9,039lb (4,100kg) dry thrust; 14,550lb (6,600kg) with afterburning.
Tactical radius: 423nm (800km).
Max. range: 1,188nm (2,200km).
Max. speed: Mach 1.06 at low level; Mach 2.2 at altitude.
Ceiling: Not known.
Armament: Air-to-air missiles, plus one 23mm twin-barrelled cannon.

In the early 1960s, the Mikoyan bureau test-flew several scaled-up versions of the MiG-21. One of these, the Ye-152A, was powered by a pair of Tumansky R-11 engines, but was never adopted for service. For its new heavy interceptor, the Soviet Air Force selected a scaled up version of the Su-9/11 series. Equipped with a nose radome and side inlets, this was deployed as the Su-15 "Flagon". Both designs seem to have been the models for China's J-8 fighter.

In the early 1970s, China flew the J-8-I, a nose-inlet aircraft powered by two 13,448lb (6,100kg) thrust Wopen 6 engines. Similar in appearance to the Ye-152A, it retained the mid-wing con-figuration of the MiG-21 rather than the low-wing scheme used on the Soviet aircraft. It proved under-powered, so only 50 to 60 were built.

To try to get the design right, the Chinese developed the aircraft into an equivalent of the Su-15 "Flagon", replacing the nose intakes with new side inlets able to admit enough air for the uprated Wopen 13 engine. In its latest 13A-II form, this engine develops 14,815lb (6,720kg) of afterburning thrust, but this is paid for in terms of engine life. Service life of the basic Wopen 13 is only 1,500hr, while time between overhauls fell from 500hr on the Wopen 13 to 300hr on the 13A-II.

In 1987, Grumman won a contract to develop a new avionics suite for the aircraft. Based on a modified APG-66 radar and a Litton LN-39 INS, this would be for use on Chinese Air Force aircraft only. Export versions would need alternative avionics.

Two aircraft were delivered to Edwards Air Force Base for flight tests of the new installation and Grumman was expected to supply 50 sets of hardware by 1995, but the deal collapsed following the attack on Chinese demonstrators at Tiananmen Square in Beijing during June 1989. The future of the F-8-II programme thus remains far from assured.

Below: The basic version of the F-8 had a MiG-21-style nose inlet and centrebody and was built in only modest quantities. It was a challenging project for the Chinese aircraft industry but hardly a front-line fighter.

Above: The definitive F-8 II has MiG-23-style side inlets and a nose radome. Under the terms of a US/Chinese agreement, Grumman was to develop a fire-control system based on the F-16's APG-66 radar.

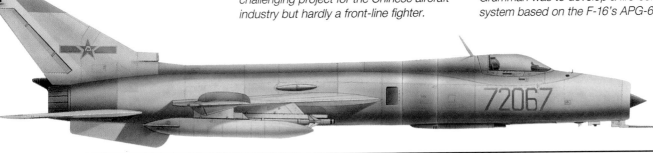

SUKHOI Su-17, -20 & -22 FITTER

A development of the Su-7 "Fitter" fighter-bomber, the Su-17/20/22 series is a classic example of the Soviet ability to wring the maximum production run and service life out of a proven design. The Su-7 had a fixed and high-swept wing, and was powered by the Lyulka AL-7 turbojet, but the new models introduced wings with variable-sweep outer sections, plus the uprated and less fuel-thirsty AL-21F-3 engine. Weapon load was doubled, range increased by almost a third and manoeuvrability was improved.

The basic Su-17 model entered service with the Soviet Air Force in 1981 and also flies with the Soviet Navy. It was followed by the Su-17M, which had a forward fuselage extended by around 10in (0.25m), a laser range-finder in the intake centrebody, plus a small undernose pod housing a Doppler navigation radar.

A newer version known to NATO as "Fitter-H" has a deepened nose in which the navigation radar is housed internally, plus a deeper and wider dorsal spine. Some are fitted with centreline sensor pods, plus under-wing fuel tanks and EW pods for use in reconnaissance roles. First seen in 1984, "Fitter-K" has a vertical fin with a small inlet for cooling air in its leading edge. Two trainer versions are known – the Su-17UM (a two-seat Su-17U) and the "Fitter-G", which is based on the "Fitter-H".

For its Warsaw Pact allies, the Soviets created the Su-20. Similar to the basic Su-17, it is powered by the Lyulka AL-21F-3 turbojet, but has downgraded avionics.

Given the widespread export success of the MiG-23, development of variants powered by the latter aircraft's Tumansky R-29 engine was an obvious move. The result was the Su-22.

This comes in at least three versions. The single-seater is similar to "Fitter-H", while the two-seater is based on "Fitter-G". Both can be recognised by a bulged rear fuselage needed to house the Tumansky engine. Final production version will probably be the Su-22M-4. Similar to "Fitter-K", this has been supplied to Czechoslovakia, East Germany and Poland.

SPECIFICATION: Su-20 "Fitter-C".
Role: Ground attack fighter.
Length: 61ft 6in (18.75m).
Height: 15ft 7in (4.75m).
Wingspan: 34ft 9in (10.6m) swept; 45ft 11in (14m) unswept.
Weights: Empty, 22,000lb (10,000kg); max. takeoff, 39,000lb (17,700kg).
Powerplant(s): One Lyulka AL-21F-3 turbojet.
Rating: 24,700lb (11,200kg) in afterburner.
Tactical radius: 340nm (630km) hi-lo-hi with 4,400lb (2,000kg) ordnance.
Max. range: Not known.
Max. speed: Mach 2.1 at altitude, Mach 1.05 at sea level.
Ceiling: 59,000ft (18,000m).
Armament: Two 30mm NR-30 cannon, plus up to 7,000lb (3,200kg) of ordnance.

Right: The Soviet Air Force's Su-17 uses a version of the Lyulka AL-21 turbojet that was fitted to the fixed-wing Su-7 and Su-9/11.

Below: Peru was an early Su-22 customer but disappointment with the simple avionics that were supplied did not deter it from buying the improved S-22M version.

SUKHOI Su-24 FENCER

First flown in the late 1960s, the Su-24 was intended to give the Soviet Union a heavy strike aircraft in the class of the USAF's F-111. The prototype had a fixed wing, but this was soon replaced by the current design. Wing sweep is not fully variable; as is the case with the smaller MiG-23, the pilot is only able to select one of three fixed settings.

The F-111 was able to use the fuel-efficient TF30 turbofan, but the Soviet Union had no engine of this type in the late 1960s and 1970s. The Su-24 therefore had to make do with the Lyulka AL-21F-3 turbojet.

At least six versions of the aircraft have been developed. The original "Fencer-A" had a rectangular section rear fuselage. This probably gave aerodynamic problems; on "Fencer-B" the rear fuselage was slimmer and faired around the jetpipes.

By the early 1980s, the standard production model was "Fencer-C", which carried better EW systems. This was soon followed by "Fencer-D", which introduced a lengthened nose, large integral fence/pylons on the glove, an EO blister aft of the nosewheel, a revised vertical fin with a kinked leading edge and an in-flight refuelling probe.

"Fencer-E" is a naval reconnaissance model which entered service in 1985, replacing the obsolete Tu-16. A new EW version reported to be under development in the late 1980s will probably be designated "Fencer-F".

The aircraft can carry conventional bombs, guided bombs and air-to-surface missiles. One six-barrelled 30mm Gatling gun is mounted in a blister fairing on the starboard side of the belly. A small fairing on the port side was formerly thought to contain a second cannon of 23mm calibre, but its true purpose remains unknown. To extend the aircraft's range, huge external fuel tanks can be carried beneath each wing glove section.

At least 900 of these variable-geometry strike fighters are in service with the Soviet Air Force and Naval Aviation. The first export order was for a batch of six aircraft that were delivered to Libya's air force in the spring of 1989.

SPECIFICATION: Su-24 "Fencer-B"
Role: Strike aircraft.
Length: 69ft 10in (21.29m).
Height: 18ft 0in (5.5m)
Wingspan: 34ft 5in (10.5m) swept; 55ft 5in (17.5m) unswept.
Weights: Empty, 42,000lb (19,000kg); loaded, 64,000lb (29,000kg); max. takeoff, 87,000lb (39,500kg).
Powerplant(s): Two Tumansky R-29B turbojets.
Rating: 17,600lb (8,000kg) dry thrust, 27,500lb (12,500kg) with afterburning.
Tactical radius: 970nm (1,800km) with two tons of ordnance plus external fuel.
Max. speed: Mach 2.1 at altitude.
Ceiling: 54,000ft (16,500m).
Armament: up to 24,000lb (11,000kg) of ordnance, plus one 30mm cannon.

Left: "Fencer-D" is a more effective aircraft than the earlier versions by virtue of better avionics plus a flight-refuelling probe.

Below: The initial "Fencer-A" model featured a square-cut aft fuselage. This gave problems in service and was replaced by a rather more sculpted design.

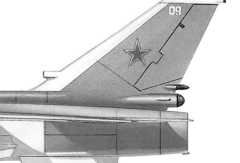

SUKHOI Su-25 FROGFOOT

SPECIFICATION: Su-25 "Frogfoot"
Role: Close support aircraft.
Length: 50ft 11in (15.53m).
Height: Not known.
Wingspan: 47ft 1in (14.36m).
Weights: Empty, 21,000lb (9,000kg); loaded, 32,187lb (14,600kg); max. takeoff, 38,800lb (17,600kg).
Powerplant(s): Two non-afterburning Tumansky R-13-300 turbojets.
Rating: 11,240lb (5,100kg).
Tactical radius: 405nm (750km).
Max. range: Not known.
Max. speed: Mach 0.7 at altitude; 475kt (880km/hr) at sea level.
Ceiling: 23,000ft (7,000m).
Armament: One cannon plus up to 9,700lb (4,400kg) of ordnance.

Left: "Frogfoot" had its baptism of fire in Afghanistan where it proved useful. Despite that, production ended in the late 1980s.

Smaller and faster than the USAF's Fairchild A-10, the Su-25 close-support aircraft was probably the last design directed by the elderly Pavel Sukhoi. The aircraft is armoured to withstand hits of up to 30mm calibre. The cockpit area is protected by titanium armour, while the engine bays are made from stainless steel. The flight control system is duplicated and the control surfaces are moved by push rods rather than cables.

Based on the Tumansky R-13 used in the MiG-21, the R-195 engine is a non-

Below: Heavy armour protection is one reason why Western engineers describe the Su-25 as being "built like a battleship".

afterburning variant able to run on aviation fuel, petrol or even diesel oil. Slotted flaps and full-span leading edge slats on the wing maximise lift potential, resulting in typical takeoff and landing runs of around the 2,000ft (600m) mark.

The 30mm twin-barrel cannon fires at up to 3,000 rounds per minute and its 250-round magazine holds enough ammunition for five one-second bursts. The underwing hardpoints can carry a total of up to 9,700lb (4,400kg) of ordnance such as 23mm gun pods, bombs, unguided rockets or laser-guided bombs. The latter can attack targets marked by the nose-mounted laser rangefinder/designator.

Two-seat trainer versions have a second cockpit with a raised seat to give the instructor an adequate forward view, but this modification gives the aircraft an ugly hump-backed appearance. To compensate for the additional side area, the vertical fin is increased in height. Some Soviet examples have an arrester hook used when teaching carrier deck landing techniques to naval pilots.

SUKHOI Su-27 FLANKER

SPECIFICATION: Su-27 "Flanker-A"
Role: Air superiority fighter.
Length: 70ft 10in (21.6m).
Height: Not known.
Wingspan: 48ft 3in (14.7m).
Weights: Empty, 37,000lb (16,800kg); loaded, 55,000lb (25,000kg); max. takeoff, 65,000lb (30,000kg).
Powerplant(s): Two Lyulka AL-31F turbofans.
Rating: c.20,000lb (9,000kg) dry thrust; c.30,000lb (13,500kg) with afterburning.
Tactical radius: 810nm (1,500km).
Max. range: Not known.
Max. speed: Mach 2.0+.
Ceiling: c.65,000ft (20,000m).
Armament: AA-8 "Aphid", AA-10 "Alamo", and AA-11 "Archer" missiles, plus a 30mm cannon.

In general appearance the Su-27 resembles the MiG-29, but the scaling up needed to create this big interceptor has created an aircraft of dramatically greater effectiveness. The original Model 1021 prototype flown in 1977 was followed by a pre-series version. This had rounded wingtips and taller tail fins, but significant redesign was needed in order to create the production fighter.

Like the smaller MiG-29, the Su-27 is equipped with both a look-down/shoot-down radar and an electro-optical search and track sensor, plus a helmet sight used for weapon aiming. The cockpit uses conventional mechanical instruments, but a digital version based on cathode-ray-tube displays is under development.

Below: The large size of the Su-27 belies an agility that is equal to that of its Western counterparts but the quality of its radar and weapons remains unknown.

Above: Sukhoi's Su-27 is the latest in a long line of heavy interceptors deployed by the Soviets to guard the skies of the homeland.

The aircraft is powered by two Lyulka AL-31F two-spool augmented turbofans, an engine in the performance class of US models such as the F100 and F110. At takeoff, these give the aircraft a thrust to weight ratio of around 1:1.

Both engines are linked to the flight-control system to ensure optimum engine performance throughout the envelope. The stunningly-dramatic pull-up manoeuvre known as "Pougachev's Cobra" seen at the aircraft's Western debut at the 1989 Paris air show confirms that the AL-31F engine can take rough handling.

The inlets are not as close to the ground as on the MiG-29, so need less protection from foreign-body ingestion. Like the smaller aircraft, the Su-27 inlets have downward swinging doors which close while the wheels are on the ground. In this case, however, the doors are made from rather coarse metal mesh.

The only other version in service is the two-seat Su-27UB, which can be used either as a trainer or as a long-range interceptor whose crew can share the workload. One development aircraft was fitted with 29,955lb (13,587kg) thrust R-32 engines (a variant of the AL-31F) and used in 1986 to set climb records. Model 1024 was a test aircraft fitted with canard foreplanes. Trials showed that the reduction in landing speed was not worth the additional complexity.

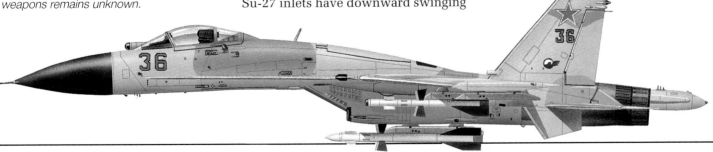

VOUGHT A-7 CORSAIR II

SPECIFICATION: A-7E Corsair II.
Role: Tactical fighter.
Length: 46ft 1.5in (14.06m).
Height: 16ft 0.75in (4.90m).
Wingspan: 38ft 9in (11.80m).
Weights: Empty, 19,127lb (8,676kg); loaded, not known; max. takeoff, 42,000lb (19,050kg).
Powerplant(s): One Allison TF41-A-2 turbofan.
Rating: 15,000lb (6,800kg).
Tactical radius: 620nm (1,150km).
Max. range: 1,981nm (3,671km).
Max. speed: 600kts (1,112km/hr) at sea level.
Ceiling: Not known.
Armament: More than 15,000lb (6,800kg) of ordnance plus one 20mm M61 cannon.

Above: Introduced during the Vietnam War, the Corsair II was a key element of carrier-borne air power in the 1980s.

This subsonic derivative of the F-8 Crusader fighter first flew in September 1965 to meet a US Navy requirement for an attack aircraft able to replace the A-4 Skyhawk. In its original A-7A form as deployed by the US Navy in 1967, the Corsair II was underpowered, but replacing the Pratt & Whitney TF30 with an Allison TF41 Spey derivative made the A-7 attractive to the USAF, which ordered 459 A-7Ds. This model was in turn navalised to create the US Navy's TF41-powered A-7E, 596 of which were eventually delivered. The USN has retired its TF30-powered aircraft but still uses the A-7E in declining numbers.

The USAF has passed its A-7Ds to the Air National Guard, which operates the A-7D alongside around 40 two-seat A-7K trainers. Just under half of the A-7D force is able to carry a Texas Instruments FLIR pod designed to display IR imagery on a GEC raster-scanned HUD, but only 110 pods were purchased. Under a programme known as LANA (Low Altitude Night Attack), 75 A-7Ds and eight A-7Ks are to get an AAR-49 FLIR, a GEC HUD and a Plessey nav/attack computer.

Two others have been rebuilt as YA-7F prototypes, receiving a longer fuselage, modified wing, leading-edge root extensions, additional internal fuel and a new engine bay able to accept an afterburning F100 or F110 engine. For trials purposes, the F100 was selected. Up to 337 ANG A-7Ds could eventually be rebuilt.

Subsonic aircraft never seem to attract the sort of orders that supersonic types do. Switzerland rejected the proposed A-7G and the only export sale was 60 A-7Hs and five TA-7Hs to Greece. The TF30-powered version is not extinct, however, Portugal using 44 A-7Ps and six TA-7Ps.

Below: Like the F-4 Phantom, the A-7 was the right aircraft at the right time, forcing the USAF to swallow its pride and "buy Navy".

YAKOVLEV Yak-38 FORGER

SPECIFICATION: Yak-38 "Forger-A"
Role: V/STOL multi-role fighter.
Length: 50ft 10in (15.5m).
Height: 14ft 4in (4.37m).
Wingspan: 24ft 0in (7.32m).
Weights: Empty, c.16,500lb (7,485kg); max. takeoff, c.25,790lb (11,700kg).
Powerplant(s): One Mikulin/Soyuz R29V-300 vectored-thrust turbojet plus two Rybinsk RD-36-35FVR lift jets.
Rating: 15,000lb (6,800kg)/6,724lb (3,050kg).
Tactical radius: 130nm (240km) lo-lo-lo.
Max. range: Not known.
Max. speed: 562kts (1,040km/hr) at low level; Mach 0.95 at altitude.
Ceiling: 39,400ft (12,000m).
Armament: Up to 7,900lb (3,600kg) of ordnance.

Above: Deployed aboard Kiev-class carriers in the late 1970s, "Forger" gave the Soviet Navy experience in flight-deck operations.

Following trials in the late 1960s with the custom-designed Yakovlev "Freehand" technology demonstrator, the prototype of this V/STOL naval fighter flew in 1971. Development seems to have been swift, with deliveries beginning in 1975.

First deployed on the carrier *Kiev* in 1976, the aircraft was modified in the light of early operating experience. Blow-in doors were fitted to the intakes, while long dorsal strakes were added to the upper fuselage. Running aft from just behind the canopy, passing on either side of the intake door for the lift jets and ending just aft of the leading-edge wing roots, these are designed to prevent engine efflux being re-ingested by the lift engines when the aircraft is in the hover.

About 75 "Forgers" had been built by the end of 1986, but few have been delivered since then. The aircraft carries only a small ranging radar, plus four underwing hardpoints for bombs, gun pods or AA-8 "Aphid" air-to-air and AS-7 "Kerry" air-to-surface missiles. Better armament, plus supersonic performance, are expected from its successor, the Yak-41.

To create the "Forger-B" two-seat trainer version, the forward fuselage was stretched by 7ft 1.75in (2.18m). The revised aircraft is about 2,000lb (907kg) heavier than the single-seater, so no radar or hardpoints are provided in order to keep takeoff weight within the capability of the existing engines.

STOL takeoffs are similar to those made by Harriers, but as well as turning the vectored thrust nozzles downwards at the appropriate point in the takeoff run, the lift engines must be brought to full thrust. Both tasks are accomplished by a fully automatic system, as are the delicate manoeuvres involved in VTOL takeoff and landing flight regimes.

Below: This early model lacks the long dorsal fences fitted on either side of the lift-jet inlets on later examples of the aircraft.

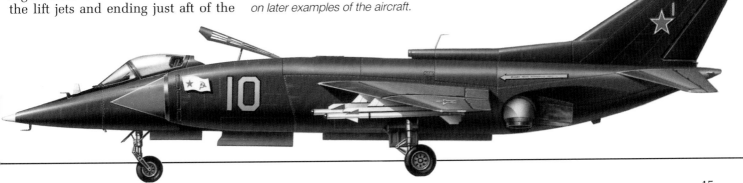

INDEX

PRINTED IN BELGIUM BY
proost
INTERNATIONAL BOOK PRODUCTION